GILES CHAPMAN

CARS ON FILM

A CELEBRATION OF CARS AT THE MOVIES

GILES CHAPMAN

CARS ON FILM

A CELEBRATION OF CARS AT THE MOVIES

The
History
Press

Front cover: A DeLorean DMC-12 in *Back to the Future: Part III.* (Alamy)

First published 2020

The History Press
97 St George's Place, Cheltenham,
Gloucestershire, GL50 3QB
www.thehistorypress.co.uk

British Library Cataloguing in Publication Data.
A catalogue record for this book is available from the British Library.

ISBN 978 0 7509 9400 2

Typesetting and origination by The History Press
Printed and bound Turkey by Imak

The Volkswagen Beetle was already a well-loved fixture of American motoring life when Disney picked one to star as the wayward Herbie in its 1968 smash hit *The Love Bug*. (Walt Disney Productions)

Showing the love: a huge parade of Beetles assembled to Berlin in 2005 pays homage to the Herbie of the film franchise, many sporting the beige paintwork, go-faster stripes and 53 racing roundel of the film original. (Volkswagen)

Obscure film stills: devoid of caption information, identifying the film – let alone the car – can be tricky. I eventually discovered this distraught couple are sitting in the Volvo 120 Amazon used in *Guilt*, a 1965 Swedish-made psychological thriller … by first deciphering the inverted logo on the steering wheel. (Svensk Filmindustri)

If you think 'influencers' are part of the modern marketing world then you should recall French actress Brigitte Bardot and her ambassadorial deal with Renault in 1959, when it launched the attractive Caravelle with her help; she was given a limitless supply for personal use, and one featured in her 1959 film *Voulez-Vous Danser Avec Moi?*. (Renault)

INTRODUCTION

This book has been a long time in preparation; about thirty-six years. It's based around my collection of rare and original film stills featuring cars of all kinds, photographic prints that I've accumulated slowly and haphazardly over that time.

In contrast to other titles that have covered the subject matter, it's not based on a wish list of well-known 'car films', car chases, or the work of specific designers building motorised props. The only criterion I've had when randomly acquiring these photographs is a car-related element to the composition – originally used to relay aspects of the story and tempt the public to buy a cinema ticket. Only when I realised my collection was several hundred strong did the concept for the book gel.

My introduction to the arcane world of the film still was an illicit one. My late aunt, Gilly Hodson, was a film publicist who worked for a London public relations company, and she was regularly the host at early-evening screenings of new releases. These were usually held in tiny, sumptuously comfortable cinemas hidden away in the basements and back alleys of Soho, where a regular cadre of film critics would avail themselves of a large gin and tonic, sink into the armchairs and watch an upcoming movie. If there was a spare seat available then I might sometimes be squeezed in too by kindly Aunt Gilly, and in such exclusive circumstances I saw films as diverse as *Beat Street*, *Greystoke: The Legend Of Tarzan* and *1984* before any other 'civilian'. As the lights went up, it was fascinating to see the faces of the audience; stony expressions meant the film was going to get a roasting in print, while animated chit-chat probably meant they grudgingly approved.

At these screenings, a press kit was usually handed out: a folder containing a resume of the plot and cast, and a clutch of black-and-white photographs for favour of inclusion with any review. I still have one of these, a striking image of French actor Christophe Lambert in *Subway* of 1985, his peroxided hair spiky above an arrogant frown, and a light sabre in his hand. Having just watched *Subway* in the cynical company of (possibly – it was dark) Barry Norman, Angie Errigo,

Derek Malcolm and Alexander Walker in 1985, the sequence that had thrilled me was Lambert driving his Peugeot 205 GTi in and out of the Paris Metro. But that didn't feature among the stills. On the other hand, in the press kit for *BMX Bandits* an MGB was shown with a stunt-cycle rider flying dramatically overhead. It was this bizarre photo that triggered my obsession for cinematic publicity where the car was called on to play its part.

I began to pick up a few more here and there at collectors' fairs and flea markets, although they've always been quite hard to find. With a new batch of films opening every single week of the year, all but the most popular were quickly forgotten. The throwaway nature of the photos and press releases issued to launch them on their way meant the accompanying bumf seemed to have little, if any, lasting value.

In the days before property prices soared, there were several scruffy shops in Soho backstreets selling film memorabilia, and some did have dusty boxes of old film stills on offer. I would rifle through them contentedly, pulling out anything with a car in it and paying a couple of pounds to take it away. Even if I had no idea what the film actually was. Of course, the search meant flicking past thousands of images of long-dead actors who never found fame in return for their decades of toil in the studios. After a couple of hours scanning them the feeling of melancholy – the sadness of what once, briefly, was – would be enough to make me run from the musty shop, gasping for breath.

And then there were always the tremendous opportunities from office clear-outs in and around Wardour Street and – quite literally – the plundering of skips as the long-redundant contents of filing cabinets were unceremoniously slung. Some of the best and rarest images in this book have been, literally, pulled from rubbish sacks when I hoped no one was looking. Undignified though this activity undoubtedly is, I take pride in my similarities to the late John Kobal. This Austrian-born film historian, and eccentric Soho character, rescued so much material from skips outside film-company offices at twilight that he became, in many cases, the sole preserver and guardian of original negatives and prints that the major Hollywood studios themselves no longer owned copies of. I believe my aunt had his phone number for whenever an office rout was due, and the Kobal Collection stands today as one of the most important film stills collections in the world.

Still more of my film/car stills have come from online auctions, often bought in large, unsorted bundles. Many of these original hard copies have had absolutely no caption information, and remained as frustrating and mysterious cinematic moments in time until countless hours using Google's image search, the Internet Movie Database and – grateful thanks for its existence – the even more specialised Internet Movie Car Database could finally prise open their identities. I've also had tremendous help from the car and film communities on Twitter (thanks in particular to the relentlessly intrepid 'detective', my colleague Ed Callow, and my friend Mick Walsh), who have helped with ID when all other efforts of mine had gone nowhere.

The pictures you'll find in this book are the result of all this occasional effort. But what exactly is a film still?

The 'stills' photographer on a production unit is an ever-present member of the team whose shots will be

In the early days of filmmaking, cost and the cumbersome nature of film cameras meant in-car driving scenes had to be shot inside the studio. Elaborately built small sets like this were used, with back-projection representing the roadscape visible to viewers in the rear and side windows. (International Museum Of Photography at George Eastman House)

In 1999, Pierce Brosnan as James Bond in *The World Is Not Enough* was typical of film stars required by the script to be seen at the wheel. In this, he drove his own mobile studio, with the film camera carefully secured into position on the car itself, in this case a suitably glamorous BMW Z8 on location in Swindon. At the time, the Z8 had not yet been revealed to the public. (BMW GB)

used to publicise the finished film. His or her work can range from scenes as they are rehearsed or performed, posed portraits on or off the set, formal or candid shots of the cast, images of the technicians at work, locations, backgrounds, props or special effects that are key to the story, and anything else deemed important to record for posterity while shooting is in progress.

Still photography is an art form in itself, albeit one rarely celebrated or recognised. In part this is because the stills photographer is obliged to represent the film as the director sees it, with obvious limitations for creative divergence. The stills have to be ready to hand out to newspapers and magazines well in advance of the film's release in cinemas, and often before the final 'cut' has been completed and, as mentioned earlier, the publicists have to pick the images they feel best represent the script, the cast, the action and the overall impression likely to convey what filmgoers can expect.

Such still photography has been part of the film industry since its beginnings, and a standard format measuring 10x8in was widespread by the 1920s. One curious aspect of them is that most feature a negative number, usually in the bottom left- or right-hand corner, that the publicist has written in tiny letters and numbers using a thin chinagraph pencil; this number usually remained during printing and so was reproduced on the actual print. The biggest change in the intervening period has probably been the availability of digital download images, which since the beginning of the twenty-first century has seen the end of producing sets of physical photographic prints.

After about 1995, the printed photograph still pretty much vanished, which is why the examples featured here are mostly confined to the twentieth century.

The level of take-up of these freely given film images in newspapers and magazines has always been extremely important to producers and studios. In print media, editorial coverage traditionally had a value four or five times the cost of equivalent advertising space, and so, even if the film gets poor reviews, the page area it garners is quantifiable as coverage. No publicity is bad publicity, even if the film itself is declared a turkey.

A fascinating side-turning to film stills are lobby cards. First distributed to movie theatres in the USA in 1913, these eight-image sets – one title card and seven scene cards – usually employed the work of film stills photographers and were sometimes intricately hand-coloured for their alternative use in display frames in cinema foyers. In a time long before the Internet, social media and photo-sharing, these cards, also measuring 10x8in and positioned at eye level around the foyer walls, were a tried and tested way to snag interest in an upcoming performance, especially if they captured the glamour, menace or humour of the film. A handful of these appear throughout the book.

Copyright in these images is an important factor, and in every case that's knowable I have attributed the film company that issued these publicity pictures. They were always meant to publicise the films they show but were only issued for that purpose on the basis they were used in an editorial context, and not co-opted to advertise other things, or to be exploited or copied for unofficial merchandise. In the file-sharing, image-swapping, digitally manipulated Internet era – that stills photographers of the 1950s and '60s would have been aghast at – these rules are flagrantly disregarded. With 'screen grabs' so easy to take, many film moments never originally intended as still images have proliferated and been widely shared all over the web. None of the images used here are unsanctioned screen grabs, though. The film companies concerned generally own the images in this book, but they are used in an entirely fair and respectful way to shine a light on the films they show. I hope the way they are presented provides a unique historical record of how cars have been portrayed in film stills, and that this in turn encourages every reader to seek out the movies and enjoy the work of all the artists who created them.

And that brings me to the films themselves. The constant temptation is always to put a value judgement on them. In all the many reference sources I've consulted to check facts, I am left with an overwhelming impression that everyone wants to be a film critic, and in doing so exhibits a cynical, world-weary, scathing discourse on the various failings they spot in (especially) older movies.

This can be a withering critique of a script, a waspish view of an individual performance, and any number of other coruscating opinions on everything from pace and continuity to picture quality and budgetary constraints. For some people, no box office hit is too big to abhor, no B-movie so cheap as to avoid sarcasm, no romance so saccharine that a sick bag isn't summoned.

I want to avoid all of that. I will agree, though, on one generality: lots of movies follow similar formats and plots, and there are many times when a high percentage of screen time devoted to cars will point to familiar scenarios. After all, you can't have a road movie without a long car journey, and high-speed chases are going to feature squealing tyres, roaring engines and, often, spectacular crashes by their very nature. Product placement by car brands can be blatant and jarring, and the symbolism of a Cadillac or a Rolls-Royce can sometimes lack subtlety. But it's all part of the cinematic world.

There isn't a film here that I haven't enjoyed watching, in full or part, in some way. I trust this collection of rare, unusual and evocative film still images makes you want to explore them too.

Opposite: Michael Deeley, who produced *The Italian Job* in 1969, said in his 2008 autobiography that it was 'the longest commercial for a car ever made'. The Mini Cooper was already a household name, of course, but the crack stunt driving team assembled by Rémy Julienne to handle the cars throughout the film did things that even the keenest Mini driver might hesitate to try. At the start of the thrilling chase sequence that defines the action-comedy movie, here are two of the cars about to descend the stairs of a Turin pedestrian underpass, egged on by extras dressed as English football supporters and directed by Peter Collinson. (Paramount Pictures)

Deeley was offered a lucrative deal by Fiat chief Gianni Agnelli to use his company's vehicles as the getaway cars. But the cheeky Britishness of the Mini Cooper was so central to the script by Troy Kennedy Martin that he was forced to decline. The production team did take advantage of the test track on the roof of Fiat's Lingotto factory; the Minis scampered around it pursued by police officers in a hapless Alfa Romeo Giulia… a car built by Fiat's main domestic rival. (Paramount Pictures)

The most dangerous stunt to pull off in *The Italian Job* was the leap from the roof of one tall building at Lingotto to another. Oddly, however, it's one of the more underwhelming sequences on-screen, and producer Deeley later said it wasn't really worth all the elaborate planning entailed. Punishing work like this was among the reasons the film crew eventually worked its way through some thirty Mini Coopers. The British Motor Corporation (BMC) had reluctantly agreed to provide six cars at cost price, so all the others had to be bought brand new from dealers before being hammered to near-destruction. 'Many of those who worked on the picture felt BMC's attitude was a sad reflection of the British car industry's marketing skills,' recalled Deeley, although the movie's charisma has helped propel Mini sales ever since. (Paramount Pictures)

The penultimate stunt in the film (the ending won't be spoiled by saying what happens next…) involved driving three Mini Coopers up a ramp into the back of a moving Bedford VAL six-wheeled coach – an extremely dangerous manoeuvre for the drivers and actors involved. It was performed on a stretch of closed motorway outside Turin as the rendition of Quincy Jones'

'The Self-Preservation Society' builds to its rousing climax on the soundtrack. *The Italian Job*, starring Michael Caine as crime gang leader Charlie Croker, who almost pulls off a massive heist of Chinese gold bullion, has time and again been voted one of the greatest British films of all time. For Mini devotees, it will always top that particular chart. (Paramount Pictures)

Two ground-down Chicago cops, played by Gregory Hines and Billy Crystal, are longing to retire and open a bar in Florida in *Running Scared* from 1986. Before they can do that they're obliged to nab one final crook, which is why they find themselves giving chase in a Chevrolet Caprice taxi to the Cadillac Deville stretch limo of a big-time drug dealer. When the Caddy swerves onto the rail tracks of Chicago's Transit Authority network, viewers are set for a stunning chase where – with one or two unconvincing inserts – the cars really do tear along the railway lines, and reportedly didn't need much modification to do so. (MGM Entertainment Co.)

The climax of the chase occurs at the LaSalle/Van Buren stop where the Cadillac ploughs head first into an oncoming train on the iconic raised-loop section of the city's metro. It's simply inconceivable anything similar would ever be allowed on the open-air parts of the London Underground, but the filming was all done for real, and is astonishingly effective. In fact, the production company bought two carriages and had them gutted, and employed Bob Janz, a CTA staff member in charge of co-ordinating filming on the Chicago network, to drive it from the third one. The Cadillac is scooped up and overturned by the train, but the chauffeur and Mr Big still make their escape, on foot. (MGM Entertainment Co.)

Ford willingly supplied as many third-generation Transits as director John Mackenzie needed for *The Fourth Protocol* in 1987. The film's star and co-producer Michael Caine is seen here on the set with one of them, talking getaway-driving techniques no doubt. The film is a fairly watchable Cold War thriller from the pen of Frederick Forsyth, and the Transit gets battered front and rear as it frees itself from traffic by ramming the cars in front of and behind it in a suspenseful traffic jam to continue giving chase. (Ford Motor Co./Rank Film Distributors)

In his efforts to head off his adversary and prevent a nuclear attack on a US air base, MI5 officer John Preston (Caine) drives the Transit like a loon including in this dust-flying moment on a motorway slip road being constructed in Chelmsford, Essex. He is out to intercept Petrofsky, who is played by Ford Escort XR3i-driving Pierce Brosnan well before the world knew him as James Bond. Brosnan had also been seen in a Jaguar XJ6 in the closing scene of *The Long Good Friday*, also directed by Mackenzie, his terrorist character holding a gun to the seething face of gangster Harold Shand (Bob Hoskins). (Ford Motor Co./ Rank Film Distributors)

Cornel Lucas's photo to launch veteran car classic *Genevieve* has it all. On the left are John Gregson and Dinah Sheridan, playing as Alan McKim and his wife Wendy, with his treasured 'Genevieve', a 1904 French-built Darracq 12hp; on the right, Kenneth More as Ambrose Culverhouse and Kay Kendall as his girlfriend Rosalind Peters with the 1904 Dutch-built Spyker. Both the cars were almost fifty years old when the film was shot in 1953. But the fact neither were British-made vehicles reflected fears from owners of Napiers and Lanchesters that they might get damaged during the intense production schedule. (Rank Organisation)

Kay Kendall gets her feet wet while Kenneth More urges her to push harder from the driving seat of the Spyker. The couple are making their way down to Brighton on the annual Veteran Car Run when they hit trouble. Director Henry Cornelius took plenty of footage of the real event in November 1952 to use convincingly throughout the movie. (Rank Organisation)

A fine turnout of both veteran cars and well-wrapped-up extras for the arrival of the Spyker at the event's finish at Marine Parade, Brighton, before the two competitive couples turn towards the capital for their ill-fated race back. The movie was shot in Technicolor, both on location and at Pinewood Studios, which was a major draw for a British film of the era. *Genevieve* is widely credited with igniting the British public's love and respect for veteran and later vintage and classic cars. (Rank Organisation)

Stills photographer Paul Bowne took this super-sharp image of stars More and Kendall in the Spyker as they bicker their way through the picture-perfect English countryside between London and Brighton. (Rank Organisation)

Kenneth More at the wheel and a jubilant-looking Kay Kendall in the passenger seat of the Spyker as the team rattles through London towards the end of the film, and their expected victory in their battle against 'Genevieve'. In the bottom right of the photo you can see the tramlines – recently made redundant after the last of the London trams was withdrawn in 1952 – in which the car became stuck, steering it away helplessly from pipping 'Genevieve' to the winning post on Westminster Bridge. (Rank Organisation)

One of the many tense moments in *Genevieve* as the tussle of the old crocks turns into a battle of the sexes. The Darracq itself had been rescued from a scrapyard in 1945 and lovingly rebuilt by Norman Reeves. He called it 'Annie' but the film script changed that to 'Genevieve' forever. A few years after the car became one of the most famous in the world, it was spirited away from the UK for a new life in the Australian collection of George and Kathleen Gilltrap. Thirty-five years later the car returned to the UK to be sold at auction, and today it's displayed in the Dutch National Motor Museum… alongside its Spyker co-star. (Brooks Auctions)

The speed freaks of *The Lively Set* are not going to be deterred by a police car – a Plymouth Savoy – blocking their drag race. On the right is Chuck Manning (Doug McClure), driving the so-called T-Bucket hot-rod, designed and built by Joe Pirronello of the San Diego Prowlers club. It was a cunning amalgam of parts from a Dodge pickup and other components from Ford Model T and Model A cars, a car that had been seen widely in specialist custom magazines in 1963. For most of the film, McClure's stunt driver double was drag-racing legend Mickey Thompson. On the left is Casey Owens (James Darren) in a roadster based on a 1929 Ford Model A. It had originally been expensively and tastefully built for an LA timber tycoon, Eddie Dye, but by the time it appeared in the film, it was much altered with a 1932 Ford radiator grille and Chevy engine. It was owned by another San Diego Prowlers member, Roger Brousseau. (Universal Pictures)

There can't be many movies in which a real car is so intrinsic to the plot, but Chrysler were intimately involved with the development of the story here because it revolved around a gas-turbine 'jet'-engined racing car. The company had just built a run of fifty of its experimental Turbine cars that were loaned out to customers in a real-life evaluation process on American roads. *The Lively Set* was the perfect way to harness Hollywood to spread the word. Leading man in this drama James Darren portrays Casey Owens, a mechanic who designs the jet car as a way to set a new land-speed record. He lands backing from wealthy Stanford Rogers (Peter Mann) but the sponsor gets cold feet when the car hits engineering snags. However,

Casey and his friend Chuck Manning (Doug McClure) keep faith in the ground-breaking new technology, and make the Turbine a winner. And here is the car itself, taking honours in the fictional Tri-State Endurance Run from LA to Las Vegas. Director Jack Arnold has created a super media circus here, but the scene is also notable for the very rare car that is following the Turbine across the finish line: a Ghia Chrysler L6.4, one of a very limited number sold to A-listers including Frank Sinatra and Dean Martin. Italy's Ghia coachworks built the bodywork for this and the fifty Turbines. Chrysler also supplied a team of designers and engineers to stunt-drive and look after the Turbine on set. (Universal Pictures)

The windscreen and steering wheel of the metallic blue 1966 Ford Thunderbird convertible give support to director Ridley Scott as his cast rehearses a scene for *Thelma & Louise* in 1991. This has become an iconic story of friendship and adventure in the vanguard of changing attitudes about what women have to put up with in men; what starts as a weekend away for two blue-collar women turns into a four-day flight for their lives. The film starred Geena Davis as Thelma, here in the back seat, and Susan Sarandon as Louise. Standing alongside her is Michael Madsen as Jimmy, Louise's musician boyfriend. (Pathe Entertainment Inc./UIP UK)

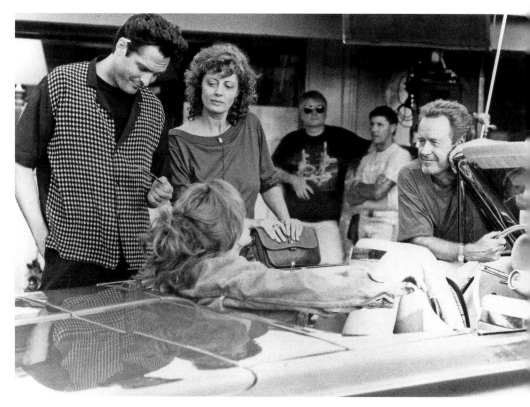

Louise Sawyer, Sarandon's character, is a put-upon coffee-shop waitress who is hoping a weekend away in her '66 soft-top Thunderbird with her best friend will be a much-needed change from the daily grind. Things change totally when they stop at a bar and she puts a bullet through the chest of an oaf who assaults and insults Thelma. From that point on, the tension and their troubles mount. No spoiler alert needed here, but suffice to say that the Thunderbird, which was a fairly desirable classic car then, could never find a way back. (Pathe Entertainment Inc./UIP UK)

The Ford Thunderbird convertible, albeit it in very slightly different 1965 guise, had a star cinematic outing the year before *Thelma & Louise*, in David Lynch's *Wild At Heart*, and in this still you can see the myriad similarities between the two cars and, of course, appreciate what an excellent vehicle it makes for filming in the brilliant light and wide open spaces of West Coast America. Nicolas Cage is Sailor Ripley, an impetuous minor criminal who, after a spell in prison, is met by his girlfriend Lula Pace Fortune, played by Laura Dern, and the convertible Ford and his treasured snakeskin jacket. They set off for a new life together in California, but in North Carolina they come across a terrible car accident where the last survivor dies in front of them, and what they don't realise is that Lula's mother has a contract out on Ripley, to remove him from her daughter's life, permanently. It won the Palme d'Or for Best Film at the 1990 Cannes Film Festival. (Palace/ Polygram Filmed Entertainment)

At least one online reviewer suggests that the best reason for watching lightweight romantic comedy *Love Is A Ball* from 1963 is indeed the car content. This still image featuring leading man Glenn Ford up to his elbows in soapsuds should be enough to convince anyone else, although the plot about the devious side of gold-digging, matchmaking and poverty-stricken aristocrats on the French Riviera is reasonably entertaining. Ford is John Lanthrop, a retired world-champion racing driver, who is recruited – against the backdrop of the 1963 Monaco Grand Prix, with some great cars and tight action – to teach a chinless marriage candidate how to control a racing car. The line-up of choice cars in this shot is (right to left): Maserati 3500GT, Rolls-Royce Silver Cloud, Bentley R-type, Facel Vega Excellence and a 1960 Cadillac. You'll see many other cars in the colour movie too, including a Mercedes-Benz 300SL roadster, Chevrolet Corvette and Renault Floride. (Gold Medal Enterprises/United Artists)

Millicent 'Milly' Mehaffey (Hope Lange, Glenn Ford's partner at the time, seventeen-year age gap notwithstanding) is the big catch in *Love Is A Ball*, based on the Lindsay Hardy novel *The Grand Duke And Mr Pimm*. Here she is trying to reconcile being a serious trainee racing driver with sprawling across the bonnet of the Maserati. The car is interesting. It was one of a pair of prototypes for an open-topped version of the 3500GT, and was shown at the 1958 Turin motor show. However, the factory decided not to sanction this Carrozzeria Touring design but the competing one from rival coachbuilder Carrozzeria Vignale, and so this red two-seater remained unique. (Gold Medal Enterprises/United Artists)

In *Slither* there is a superb cast of characters in a quirky and anarchic road movie that's a cut above the slapstick usual. James Caan as Dick Kanipsia is an ex-con who gets caught up in the quest for a haul of stolen cash, hooking up with a variety of weirdos as he staggers around trying to get his hands on it. Chief among these is Sally Kellerman's Kitty Kopetsky, a bunny-boiler freak who does all she can to get one over on her shambolic travelling companion, while never actually deserting her. The two of them are here in her 1972 Chevrolet Impala Sport Sedan towing an Airstream California trailer caravan as a sinister 'recreational vehicle' – which has been tailing them from a rundown campsite – tries to force them off the road. (Metro-Goldwyn-Mayer)

One of the matt-black vans belonging to the mysterious mob in *Slither* meets a messy end by splashing down into a cesspit as it tries to evade a roadblock. The vehicle seems to be falling apart in mid-air even before it makes its smelly splashdown. Although it resembles a weird, four-wheeled aardvark that looks custom-created for the part, it was actually a real production vehicle, a 1971/72 RecTrans Discoverer 25R mobile home. It weighed 5 tons despite carrying a glass-fibre body, and there was just one door on the side to enter and exit the vehicle. Two of them appear in this now-obscure but highly enjoyable film. (Metro-Goldwyn-Mayer)

Bill Travers at the wheel and Sid James in the passenger seat of a 1958 Lister-Jaguar sports-racer, the three main attractions in the 1961 British motor-racing movie *The Green Helmet*. The 180mph car itself, with its wind-cheating, Frank Costin-designed aluminium body, had been driven in real life by Formula 1 hero Archie Scott-Brown, and even competed at Le Mans, before being sold on in 1959 and eventually being picked for its role in the film, where its registration number VPP 9 was carefully masked. In fact, two similar cars were used after the first was damaged while shooting, leading to a couple of continuity mess-ups. (MGM)

It's hard to know whether this crash damage to the Lister-Jaguar being dolefully studied by Bill Travers was from the real shunt that happened during the making of *The Green Helmet*, or was mocked-up by the film crew for a crucial moment of drama in the script. The film was based on a bestselling book of the same name by Australian novelist Jon Cleary, who wrote it in just twenty days, and although he set a lot of it in Italy, most of the location work was done in Wales. (MGM)

Among the stills issued to announce *The Green Helmet* was this highly dramatic shot of a Porsche 718 RSK at the start of a horrific-looking barrel-roll at the Eau Rouge circuit, Spa-Francorchamps in Belgium. It wasn't shot by the crew but was a film insert of a real accident that happened in 1959. Remarkably the driver Bino Heims was thrown clear of the wreckage and staggered away largely unhurt, which meant the footage could be used without any accusations of bad taste. (MGM)

Another scene from *The Green Helmet*, this time featuring the rather tamer charms of a Triumph Herald convertible. The film was the last non-comedy role taken by Sid James, seen here on the left, before he was lost to the *Carry On...* series and TV sitcoms. Although James was South African, director Michael Furlong insisted he adopt the Australian accent of his race-mechanic character, leading to tiresome repetition of 'sport'. Fortunately, however, real Australian racing legend Jack Brabham is part of the cast. Also in this photo are Ursula Jeans (far right) as Mrs Rafferty and Nancy Walters as Diane, the leading man's love interest. (MGM)

In Warsaw, disturbed young drifter Jacek Łazar (Mirosłav Baka) just happens to flag down the taxi of greedy, lascivious and repellent cab driver Waldemar Rekowski (Jan Tesarz). The car is unusual for international audiences but very common in Poland. It's an FSO Polonez 1500, a five-door hatchback known as a workhorse in its native country. When Jacek loses it, he attacks Waldemar, but it takes two attempts to finish him off. Then, after he's dumped the body in a river and taken the FSO himself, his very first fare has a suspicion she's seen the car before. *A Short Film About Dying* is gruesome but gripping. (Pathe Releasing Ltd)

In Britain's motorway-building boom of the 1960s and '70s, there were always plenty of unopened slip roads or half-finished junctions with expansive empty tarmac on which stunts and car chases could be staged by film-makers to dramatic effect, if not total reality. This humdrum location is just such a spot in Bracknell, Berkshire, where the newly laid landscaping turf is also taking a bashing during filming of Richard Burton's gangster film *Villain* in 1971. As part of a planned assault on the payroll of a plastics factory, the Vanden Plas 3-Litre on the right is being pursued by the gang working for Vic Dakin (Burton) in a Ford Zodiac MkIV-style Executive, and shortly after the tyre squealing died down the Vanden Plas was rammed T-bone style by a stolen Jaguar S-type. (Anglo-EMI/MGM-EMI)

The ambush takes a nerve-wracking wrong turn in this still snatched from the heist scene in *Villain*; the car being chased manages to pull away, leading the hoodlums' Ford Executive to reverse straight into the gang's Triumph 2000 back-up car. Burton delivers a snarlingly nasty portrayal of an ageing gangland boss losing control, with Ian McShane as his bisexual lover Wolfe Lissner, and some choice Cockney one-liners. With its overtones of the Kray brothers' saga and a grim, crumbling London underworld, it's a very violent film, gratuitously so many thought at the time, but the gritty premise fed into the realism of TV police drama *The Sweeney*, as did the tendency to smash up large, second-hand British saloon cars in pursuits and shunts on authentic city streets. (Anglo-EMI/MGM-EMI)

'Spoof' is a word that could have been invented for Panthers, which were usually loose replicas of great classic cars of the past. In the case of the Panther Deville, it was a none-too-accurate yet still spectacular reinterpretation of the Bugatti Royale. A Deville four-door saloon is here, then, brought into action for another kind of spoof James Bond with a female protagonist. *The Golden Lady* is about a team of elite female mercenaries hired to eliminate rivals to Britain in a bidding war for access to oil fields in the fictional emirate of Kubran. There is, of course, plenty of double-crossing among the gold lamé, disco soundtrack, primitive computer kit and karate kicks. Shown here in a mistressful fight scene is brigade leader Julia Hemingway, who was portrayed in the 1978 film by Iva Skriver, a Danish actress credited under the name 'Christina World'... so the movie's producers could claim Miss World was in their picture. Neither soft porn nor gripping thriller, it was directed by Spanish low-budget movie cult figure José Ramon Larraz, who at least puts a bit of spirit into the Panther's highlight car chase, alongside the cheesy seduction and spying. (Elcotglade/Target International Pictures)

Above left: Britain's Panther Car Company was notable for the theatricality of the cars it produced over its relatively short period in business, so these bespoke products of Robert Jankel's Weybridge-based car factory found a natural place in front of the camera. Here, for example, is cocksure leading man Nicky Henson at the wheel of the model that launched Panther in 1972, the J72 evocation of the immortal SS 100 Jaguar sports car of the 1930s.

Henson is in his element here as Charles Bind in *Number One Of The Secret Service*, an action-comedy calculated by its Canadian writer and director Lindsay Shonteff to exploit the popularity of the James Bond franchise. The car's registration number reveals it as the demo car property of London Panther dealer HR Owen, which was no doubt delighted to see the expensive J72 on-screen. (Lindsay Shonteff Film Productions/Hemdale)

Above right: The most high-profile movie outing without doubt for any Panther was in *101 Dalmatians* in 1996, starring Glenn Close as brilliantly nasty Cruella De Vil. It was a live-action reprise of the classic Disney animated film of 1961, with its saga of spotted-dog-napping and fur coats. While the producers were casting around for a sinister-looking, long-bonneted 1930s car for Close's lead character, amusingly they found the Panther Deville

would be just the job. It's in the background in this still by Clive Coote. A modified two-door model appears throughout both this 1996 film and its 2000 sequel, *102 Dalmatians*. You may also like Hugh Laurie and Mark Williams as De Vil's inept henchmen Jasper and Horace, who carry out her dastardly orders with the help of what, today, would be quite a rare Ford Transit MkII pickup. (Disney Enterprises Inc)

If you can picture an early-1970s computer then you can imagine a machine the size of a house was needed to calculate the crucial figure for this stunt. And that was 41: 41mph was the exact speed Lauren Willert needed to travel at in an American Motors Corporation Hornet hatchback before hitting the take-off ramp. In doing so he hoped to pull off the world's first 'astro spiral' stunt – a mid-air barrel-roll jump – to get safely across this river in *The Man With The Golden Gun*, the 1974 James Bond box office smash. Boffins tapped in all the relevant data, including the weight, aerodynamics and length of the orange car, the precise trajectory, and the 50ft height above the water. The calculation printout confirmed it was going to be possible, with just one fallible element – the human factor. And that was all down to stuntman Lauren 'Bumps' Willert, with ambulances, nurses, doctors, skin divers and a crane all standing by at the location near Bangkok, Thailand. 'It is a hell of a gamble,' said 38-year-old Willert. But he did it, and afterwards the crew celebrated with champagne and Willert got a $1,000 bonus. The single-take scene shown in this sequence, lasting all of ten seconds, took £120,000 of the film's budget but it was, according to co-producer Cubby Broccoli, 'worth every Goddamn dime'. Roger Moore said at the time he'd have liked a go at it, although of course the insurers would never have allowed it. Willert, meanwhile, gave up his stunt career shortly afterwards, subsequently spending twenty-five years as a US truck driver. (Syndication International)

Left: The very next movie Mark Hamill made after the unexpected phenomenon of *Star Wars* in 1977 was *Corvette Summer*, and here he is with his co-star Annie Potts and the long-bonneted all-American sports car that's the centrepiece of this well-liked romantic drama. It raised $35m at the box office and 'Luke Skywalker' has always spoken well of the film, while pointing out that it's actually a touching love story rather than a festival of horsepower. Hamill's Kenny Dauntley is a Californian high-school major who builds a one-off customised 1973 Corvette Stingray as a shop class project with fellow students. As well as giving the car a startling new nose section, wide magnesium wheels, side exhaust pipes and a wild candy apple metal-flake paintjob complete with flames licking around the wheel arches, the class converts it from left- to right-hand drive. This is to make the car perfect for cruising along while admiring the girls on the sidewalk. Not so much kerb crawling as an outlet for teenage exuberance. In fact, the car is such a gem when it's finished that it's stolen almost immediately… (Metro-Goldwyn-Mayer)

Right: In his efforts to get his beloved Corvette back, Kenny Dauntley (Hamill) heads for Las Vegas on reports that that's where it's been taken. On the way, he hooks up with an amateur hooker called Vanessa (Potts). Having finally tracked the car down to a crooked garage owner, Kenny is dismayed to find his teacher Ed McGrath – desperate for money – had a shameful part in the Corvette's theft. Here Kenny is yanking Jeff (Brion James), a car wash worker with the Corvette's thief, from the stolen car. But getting it back again is no easy task. MGM had two doppelganger Corvettes specially built for the filming of *Corvette Summer* by Korky's Kustom Studios. Both were later sold and survive in private hands, while the mould for the cars' unique frontage is now in the custodianship of the National Corvette Museum in Kentucky. (Metro-Goldwyn-Mayer)

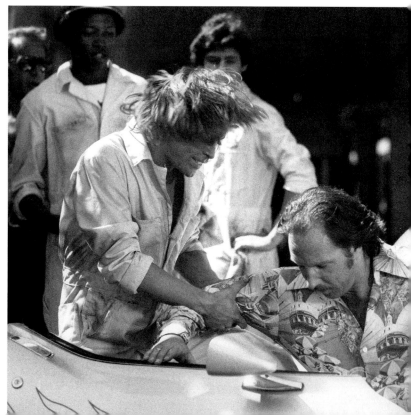

Left: This group is a cluster of very un-James Bond James Bond cars at variance with the usual high-performance machinery with which Ian Fleming's suave agent is associated. Indeed, just for a change, the decision was taken to leave the Aston Martin DB5 out of this book, as it's probably the most high-profile 007 machine and almost boringly familiar. What contrast, then, to this humble Citroën 2CV6 in *For Your Eyes Only*, in which Bond (Roger Moore) and Melina Havelock (Carole Bouquet) have a white-knuckle escape ride down the tight hillside roads of Madrid; the actual film location in 1981 was Corfu in Greece and the 2CV6 had a more powerful engine from the Citroën GS to cope with the caning. (Citroën Cars)

Right: Roger Moore is notably dapper in this still from *Moonraker*, where he's posing with the MP Lafer sports car that his contact in Rio, Manuela (Emily Bolton), uses to tail him soon after he arrives in the early scenes of the 1979 007 outing. The Lafer was a Brazilian-built replica of Britain's MG TD of the late 1940s, with a glass-fibre body over the recycled chassis of a Volkswagen Beetle. Over its sixteen years on sale between 1974 and 1990, some 4,300 examples were made in São Paolo, and today the car itself is quite coveted as one of a handful of Brazilian classics. Bond, though, does not actually drive it. (Eon Productions/United Artists)

Left: Audi was a willing supplier of cars to the production team on *The Living Daylights* in 1987. The first time 007 (Timothy Dalton) drives one is in Bratislava when he uses a range-topping 200 Quattro belonging to British Intelligence's Station V in Vienna to speed General Georgi Koskov (Jeroen Krabbé) away from the Slovakian capital; Audi has this car in its historic collection, although it's rarely shown in public. Then we have Bond driving this Audi 200 Avant Quattro in Tangier, Morocco, to follow KGB head Pushkin (Jonathan Rhys-Davies) to the Hotel Ile De France. Both Audis were certainly ideal for travelling incognito. (Eon Productions/Audi UK)

It's easy to forget that, before he plunged into Shakespearean theatre and then became a 1980s TV sitcom fixture (and subject of relentless parody as a rich-toned luvvie on *Spitting Image*) Donald Sinden was a major 1950s film star, awarded a seven-year contract with the Rank Organisation at Pinewood Studios. His most well-known appearances were in *The Cruel Sea* and several *Doctor...* films but here he is as the decidedly anxious Peter Weston, a man who gets lumbered with an abandoned reptile that he can't seem to shake off. In this still by Harry Gillard, Sinden is arriving home at the wheel of an absolutely pukka vintage sports car, a green 1928 Lagonda 2-litre low-chassis tourer. Its registration number PK 9201 marked it out as one of the four-car Fox & Nicholl racing team that campaigned in the 1929 season. Made in 1955, *An Alligator Named Daisy* was a very well-reviewed comedy with a great cast including Diana Dors and Margaret Rutherford. (Rank Organisation)

Another actor much loved for his radio and TV quiz shows, but really not much for his minor film roles, was Nicholas Parsons, who has scrawled his autograph over this still of himself in character. The movie is *Brothers In Law*. Made in 1957 by Roy Boulting, it was a satire on the world of the legal profession. The future host of *Just A Minute* is Charles Poole, a fellow tenant at a house where young barristers Ian Carmichael and Richard Attenborough find lodgings, and owner of this decrepit-looking car. The producers wanted something Parsons could be seen tarting up at the roadside with a tin of red paint. They reckoned this heap, found in Ireland, with an Austin Seven chassis and Ford side-valve engine, would do. No one then could have known what an astoundingly important car it actually was: it's the Lotus Mk2, the second car hand-built by Lotus founder Colin Chapman in 1947/8, and fitted with a natty lowered bonnet line and sloping nose cone. He used it in speed trials, where in 1950 it beat the pants off a Bugatti Type 57, and then it became the very first Lotus ever sold by Chapman to a customer – in this case Mike Lawson, uncle to Stirling Moss. At the end of the film, the car restored, Parsons uses it to whisk away his fiancée, but the car itself ended up forgotten in pieces for twenty-two years in a shed, from where it was rescued in 1989 and has been highly cherished ever since. (British Lion Films)

Michael Gothard and Judy Bloom about to play a grisly scene in the 1970 British horror film *Scream And Scream Again*. Among fans of the genre this movie has a special kudos, being the first time that horror greats Vincent Price, Peter Cushing and Christopher Lee were all cast in the same piece together. Among its several creepy storyline strands is Gothard's Keith and his penchant for leaving nightclubs with beautiful girls who succumb to his blood-sucking fetish, including Bloom's Helen Bradford here in the passenger seat of his 1955 Austin-Healey 100/4. (Amicus/American International)

Tracked down and found in the undergrowth, Detective Constable Griffin (Julian Holloway) grabs the dastardly Keith, with blood dribbling from his lips. But four burly coppers are not enough to stop him making his escape in the Austin-Healey, and so begins an extraordinarily long – for a British film – car chase. Arranging it was credited to stuntman Joe Dunham, who donned lilac shirt and wig to impersonate Keith while he also undertook the driving itself. Close scrutiny of the chase reveals that director Gordon Hessler mixed footage shot on the open road with action sequences filmed at the track of the Military Vehicles & Engineering Establishment at Chertsey, Surrey, a closed circuit free of public traffic that's used by everyone from trainee tank drivers to car magazine photographers. (Amicus/American International)

Left: In *Blue Ice* Michael Caine is a jazz club owner but also a former spy who finds himself drawn out of retirement and lured back into the espionage world. The modest, London-set thriller actually gets going when Caine's Jaguar XK150 – complete with CD player for some hepcat sounds – is rear-ended by Sean Young, in this R107-type Mercedes-Benz SL. As you can see, they're soon entwined, but for Caine's character of Harry Anders there's much more in store than a visit to the crash-repair centre. (Guild Film Distributors Ltd)

Below: Struggling widow, single parent and English teacher Nora McPhee (Marsha Mason) is shocked to find a gleaming new Mercedes-Benz SL outside her rundown LA home. It's yet another gift from a man who's turned up claiming to be her long-lost father Max; he's been on the run from prison for years and wants to pass on some of the money he embezzled from a Las Vegas casino before he dies. As she keeps refusing to accept it, the Merc and a host of expensive household appliances are how he starts to gift it to her. Released in 1983, the Neil Simon-penned comedy *Max Dugan Returns* received good reviews, and is notable as the film debut for both Matthew Broderick, seen here as Marsha's son Michael, and also Keifer Sutherland. (Twentieth Century Fox Film Corp)

The parlous state of the 1970s British film industry was very slightly alleviated by a slew of comedy films based on popular television sitcoms from the BBC and, mainly, ITV. There were few bigger mid-week family laughs than *Bless This House* and so it was a perfect candidate for the big screen upgrade with, naturally, *Bless This House* in 1972. Sid Abbott (Sid James), earthy stationery salesman from suburban Putney with perplexing teenage kids, comes up against his snooty new neighbour Ronald Baines (Terry Scott). In their ongoing wrangles, director Gerald Thomas staged this not-entirely-convincing parking altercation, in which Sid's Ford Cortina MkIII estate has dislodged the headlamp bezel of Ronald's Vauxhall Viscount; curiously, the scene was deleted from the final cut. (Rank Film Distributors)

After an exploding whisky still and a burning garden shed, the climax of *Bless This House* is a last-minute dash to the church for the wedding of Sid's son Mike (Robin Askwith) to Ronald's daughter Kate (Carol Hawkins). In their morning suits and toppers with fire-blackened faces, they hitch a lift to a happy ending clinging to the back of a fire engine, which is a 1953 Bedford SHZ very similar to the Army's familiar 'Green Goddess' fire appliances. The two middle-aged stars did their own 'stunt riding' in this scene, filmed on Burnham High Street in Buckinghamshire. (Rank Film Distributors)

Impatient advertising executive Neal Page (Steve Martin) has been punched in the face by the airport cab dispatcher just as shower-curtain ring salesman Del Griffiths (John Candy) turns up with the car that he hopes will get them both home for Christmas. Joyce Rudolph was the stills photographer for this photo. *Planes, Trains And Automobiles* of 1987 is one of the funniest, yet ultimately most touching, comedies of all time, a tale of two mismatched travelling companions battling everything that America's transport system can throw at them. Del's rental car is a 1986 Chrysler Town & Country convertible, the ultimate incarnation of the front-wheel drive K-Car series that is credited with saving Chrysler Corporation from bankruptcy. (Paramount Pictures Corporation)

Through some hair-raising driving manoeuvres directed by John Hughes, who also wrote and produced *Planes, Trains And Automobiles*, the Town & Country takes a fair battering, losing its hood, its fake woodgrain side panels peeling off, and the interior being burnt to a crisp. In this image, taken again by Joyce Randolph, Del has just delivered the immortal line, 'I know it's not pretty to look at but it'll get you where you want to go,' to a horrified traffic cop. Although, shortly afterwards, the creaking Chrysler does reach the end of its road. With its 2.6-litre Mitsubishi four-cylinder engine, the elaborately decorated convertible wasn't particularly powerful, with a feeble 96bhp on tap. But it was a rare car, with fewer than 5,000 examples sold between 1982 and '86. (Paramount Pictures Corporation)

Left: The menacing visage of the 1957 Plymouth Fury is perfectly captured in this still image to market *Christine* – with blazing headlights and angry red paint, it featured in the impactful poster for the 1983 film version of Stephen King's novel. It was a big hit that year. The film version differs slightly from King's plot in that, on-screen, the car shows its deadly vengefulness before it's even rolled off the production line at Chrysler's factory in September 1957, whereas the book explains its evil nature comes from its previous owner. (Columbia-EMI-Warner Distributors)

Right: Arnie (Keith Gordon) and girlfriend Leigh (Alexandra Paul) are aghast at the damage wreaked on Christine, even down to the badly distorted tailfins. Director John Carpenter had to scour California for cars to use in the film, and eventually found twenty-four of them at a time when the '57 Fury was already becoming very collectable. Quite a number were wrecks already, and many were the similar-looking but less valuable Plymouth Belvedere and Savoy models that were then carefully dressed to resemble the Fury. Yet another issue was that most Furys were originally painted beige, whereas the film cars all needed to be red and white. Many were completely destroyed during filming. Christine was able to repair herself on-screen – no CGI existed – because the fantastically inventive special-effects team used hydraulic pistons to crumple bodywork sections from within, and then editors reversed the film footage… (Columbia-EMI-Warner Distributors)

Solitary teenager Arnie Cunningham buys the Plymouth twenty-one years after she was built, and restores her from a tatty wreck to good-as-new condition. In symbiosis, Christine takes stealthy control of Arnie's shy personality, moulding him to her late 1950s rock 'n' roll mindset. When school bullies Vandenburg, Buddy and Moochie decided to wreck Arnie's pride and joy – seen here in full vandalism swing – Arnie is distraught. But Christine repairs herself, and then sneaks off at night to track down and kill her attackers. From there on, anyone who takes Arnie away from her had better run from the threatening burble of a hemi-head V8 engine. (Columbia-EMI-Warner Distributors)

Michael Caine (left) and Nigel Davenport (right) are seen here setting off across the North African desert, an oil-industry worker and a convicted criminal reluctantly united in a mission to destroy a German Afrika Korps fuel depot in the gritty WWII actioner *Play Dirty*, released in 1969. Their transport, naturally, is a ruggedly equipped Willys Jeep. After plans foundered to shoot in Israel and then Algeria or Morocco, the filming was done in Almeria, Spain. It was a frustrating business because the location was being used by another crew making a 'spaghetti western', which meant tank tracks carefully laid into the sand were constantly obliterated by hoof marks and piles of horse manure. (United Artists Corporation)

Another 1969 film still, from *The Sterile Cuckoo*, with another Willys Jeep at exactly the same angle, but the scenario couldn't be further removed from 'Desert Rats' warfare. The story is about two teenagers, the eccentric Mary-Ann 'Pookie' Adams, played by Liza Minnelli, and the shy Jerry Payne (Wendell Burton), who meet on a bus on the way to starting college in New York. They fall for each other but the twists and turns of their relationship become a bit overpowering; Pookie's face as Jerry leaves his quirky girlfriend for some light relief with friends betrays the pain she fears at parting. Check out the bonnet-less Jeep with whitewall tyres, classic cheap student transport of the time. (Paramount Pictures Corporation)

George Barris was widely revered as king of the Hollywood customisers – the go-to guy if a film or script or character demanded a car like no other. While his most high-profile creations were outrageous vehicles like the Batmobile and Pink Panther car for television shows, he would turn his hand to anything required. In the case of *National Lampoon's Vacation* in 1983, this was a rolling skit on the typical ugly, over-bodied and elaborate American family car of the late 1970s. As this might have offended real-life manufacturers, Barris heavily disguised a 1979 Ford LTD Country Squire station wagon and turned it into the 'Wagon Queen Family Truckster', complete with eight headlamps, imitation wood panels over garish avocado paintwork, a bizarre fuel filler flap and an airbag made from a bin liner. It meets this sorry end in a crash near Monument Valley in the Arizona desert although ever-positive family head Clark Griswold (Chevy Chase, standing on the roof) doesn't let even this calamity get him down. (Warner Bros)

In *National Lampoon's Vacation* the accident-prone Griswold family are on a 'bonding' road trip from Chicago to California, travelling in the new family car rather than flying. At several points on the cross-country journey Clark is admired by a mysterious woman driving a red Ferrari 308 GTSi. She doesn't even have a name in the script but is played by former supermodel and sometime actress Christie Brinkley. In this gag-packed comedy, she and Clark meet up at a hotel en route and enjoy a bit of skinny-dipping – about as likely a scenario as just about everything else here. (Warner Bros)

Left: Chris Rea's simple premise, of a childhood fascination with motor racing and the impact the death of a hero can make on a young mind, was turned into a filmic fantasy in 1996 for *La Passione*, accompanied by lovingly researched archive inserts and the rock musician's own score. Shirley Bassey, shown here, lent both her voice and her presence to the piece. Partly inspired by Rea's own early life in the north-east of England, it was meant to represent the imagination and escapism fired at some point in every kid, although Warner Brothers viewed it more as evocative moving wallpaper for Rea's songs in the company's first music DVD release. In the background to this scene is a replica of a 1961 Ferrari 250 TR161 Le Mans car that Rea commissioned for use in the film, using the basis of a Ferrari 330 road car as it was the closest to the real thing in dimensions like wheelbase, chassis and engine position. (East West)

Below: German racing driver Wolfgang Von Trips was celebrated in *La Passione*. He was driving a Ferrari Tipo 156 'shark-nose' Formula 1 car in the 1961 Italian Grand Prix when he fatally crashed, robbing the motor-sport world of one of its most charismatic and talented drivers. None of the original cars built in 1961 and '62 survives and so Chris Rea, as the writer, producer and driving force of this very personal project, had this close copy built, using a Fiat Dino V6 engine. (East West)

Above left: You may never have guessed that a 1978 movie about American trucking, cashing in on the then-massive craze of Citizen's Band (CB) radio, was entirely British backed. Nor, perhaps, that despite many hostile reviews, *Convoy* recouped its $12m budget nearly twice over and made the US box office Top 10. It was the sort of dream commercial breakthrough EMI had longed for in the States. The story revolves around Kris Kristofferson, the trucker with the famous 'Rubber Duck' call sign, and his vendetta with a sheriff out to destroy his reputation as an eighteen-wheeled titan of the highway. One of the film's highlights is a mile-long convoy of trucks, given cinematic splendour in aerial footage from which this still was taken. (EMI Films)

Above right: *Convoy's* plot drew on the lyrics of the 1975 country and western novelty hit single of the same name by CW McCall, fleshed out into a screenplay by BWL Norton. In this guise, as predominantly an action film, the love interest is provided by Ali McGraw. In the spectacular opening scene, she roars past The Duck in his articulated Mack tanker driving this Jaguar XK-E, or E-type Series III V12 as it was better known outside the US. Toying with each other, the two drivers almost cause a head-on collision with a police car, setting up the premise for the whole film. The Jag conks out and has to be sold, so Ali's Melissa then hitches her fortunes to the bearded trucker for the rest of the cargo-hauling action. (EMI Films)

The director Ken Annakin is quoted as saying, 'The automobiles should give me a good 30 per cent of the comedy,' about the four-wheeled stars of his 1969 screwball adventure *Monte Carlo Or Bust!*, set around a 1920s international car race. He wrote and helmed the film as a sequel to his hugely popular *Those Magnificent Men In Their Flying Machines* of four years earlier, and in the USA it was released with the chiming but clunky title *Those Daring Young Men In Their Jaunty Jalopies*.

The ambitious filming schedule took the crew all over Europe in March–May 1968, including Swedish ski slopes where a team of six stuntmen stood in for the all-star cast. A plastic replica of the 1928 Lea Francis 12/40 P-Type used was built for the rigours of filming, such as in this dramatic ski-lift scene, while an AC Cobra chassis was used for a copy of a Mercedes-Benz SSK that could take a pasting from the stunt drivers throughout the long filming schedule. (Paramount Pictures)

Here featured in a 1969 press photo call in London to publicise *Monte Carlo Or Bust!/Those Daring Young Men In Their Jaunty Jalopies*, the real 1928 Lea Francis 12/40 P-Type shows off its many ingenious features. In the film the car is driven by comedy double-act Peter Cook and Dudley Moore as Major Dawlish and Lieutenant Barrington respectively, advertising many of their patented inventions including the Dawlish Klaxon, the Dawlish Periscope, the Dawlish Snow-Stoppers and the Dawlish Extending Foglamp. Oh, and some rocket boosters too. Other great pairings were Terry-Thomas and Eric Sykes in a renamed Morris Oxford 'Bullnose', and Italian character actors Walter Chiari and Lando Buzzanca as sex-mad Angelo and Marcello campaigning a Lancia Lambda. (Author's collection)

The central thread, and source of many jokes, is the private battle for victory waged between Terry-Thomas's caddish Sir Cuthbert Ware-Armitage in his Nifty Nine MkII and Tony Curtis as American Chester Scofield in the Triple S Six-Cylinder Special (a thinly disguised Alvis Speed 20). Sourcing the cars for the film was entrusted to a former racing driver, David Watson, and it seems he picked models appropriate to each character, even minor ones like Dominique (Nicoletta Machiavelli) who was equipped with this cute Peugeot 201. The cars were modified in Italy by tuning firm Giannini Automobili, whose workshops were not far from the Rome studio where the film was based, although this accounted for but a small part of the lavish $10m budget. In the early 1970s the film was sometimes re-released in cinemas as a double bill with *The Italian Job* – a feast for all popcorn-munching car buffs. (Paramount Pictures)

Grace Kelly receives a little adjustment for hair and make-up in this candid still from the set of *High Society*, the 1956 jazz-infused musical comedy, as Frank Sinatra looks on. Well, filming in any open car is bound to take its toll, however minor, on beauty, and this was Kelly's final film role before becoming full-time royalty in Monaco. She is at the wheel of her appropriately glamorous Mercedes-Benz 190SL. As Mike Connor, Sinatra is the gossip-magazine reporter falling in love with the woman whose upcoming wedding he is supposed to be covering, while Kelly's Tracy Lord is the dazzling socialite torn between her ex-husband, her fiancé (Bing Crosby as musician Dexter Haven) and Sinatra's charismatic interloper. (Metro-Goldwyn-Mayer)

High Society was filmed mostly around Rhode Island, it's said to take advantage of the Newport Jazz Festival taking place at the same time there. Although the scene with Kelly and Sinatra was fairly short, Mercedes-Benz's US importer Max Hoffmann must have been thrilled that its stylish two-seater roadster on display at his New York showrooms had been chosen to share screen time with the three legends in the main roles. Some sources claim the car was Kelly's own, and she was certainly known as a keen driver. Although the 300SL was a bigger and much more powerful car, it gained a notoriety throughout Hollywood for being just too hot to handle; stars from Steve McQueen to Ava Gardner were involved in crashes in theirs that nearly ended careers. (Daimler-Benz AG)

Left: In the 1950s and '60s, no one in the British car industry was quicker off the mark for tabloid-friendly public relations than the Rootes Group, makers of several brands of car that generally needed all the help they could get to compete with more dynamic rivals. If a big star was in town then their Piccadilly PR office would leap into action, as here in 1966 when a Humber Super Snipe was on hand to deliver a 20-year-old Liza Minnelli to Pinewood Studios, and other locations, while she was making *Charlie Bubbles*. (Rootes Group)

Below left: Rootes was just as much on the case in the US as in Britain. Its Sunbeam Tiger was specially designed with a powerful Ford V8 engine to have appeal on the West Coast and in the sunshine states. So it would never do any harm to loan one to Hollywood Legend Cary Grant, and let everyone see him drive off the set to lunch in it. (Rootes Group)

Below right: It's the 1958 London Motor Show at the Earl's Court Exhibition Centre, and the Rootes car benefiting from some celebrity stardust is a Singer Gazelle convertible. No doubt it was an attractive couple of hours' lolly for gap-toothed comedy film actor Terry-Thomas to grin and chortle for the press photographers on press day. With him is actress Penny Morrell, later married to George Cole. A couple of years later Thomas starred in *School For Scoundrels* alongside an Aston Martin DB3S, an Austin-Healey 100/4 and the infamous '1924 Swiftmobile', a heavily disguised 1928 Bentley 4.5-litre. (Rootes Group)

The actor on the left you'll probably recognise as Donald Pleasence, here in the part of Lucas Deranian, fixer/lawyer to the scheming millionaire Aristotle Bolt (Ray Milland) in the 1975 Disney children's classic *Escape To Witch Mountain*. The bear he's encountering, though, you've probably seen just as many times without realising it. This is Bruno, a showbiz regular throughout his nineteen-year life with over 400 TV appearances alone. The American black bear, despite weighing 650lb, was trained to be gentle with children (although there is something appalling in the way his teeth and claws had been removed early on). Here he is in the commodious passenger seat of Deranian's gleaming 1974 Lincoln Continental MkIV. He needed to be docile in the film as its two stars were themselves children. Ike Eisenmann and Kim Richards portrayed mysterious orphan siblings Tony and Tia Malone. Their amazing powers were sought by Bolt in his quest to understand the paranormal, but the kids don't intend to be kept prisoners in his castle, no matter what the trappings. (Walt Disney Productions)

Disney's special effects team had a field day with *Escape To Witch Mountain*. The children come to understand that, despite distant memories of being rescued at sea, they are actually aliens from another planet, and Tony's special powers include the psychokinetic ability to animate and control objects. After they escape Bolt's hideaway, they go on the run, and are helped to stay hidden by grumpy widower Jason O'Day (Eddie Albert). They head for Witch Mountain in his green-and-white motorhome, which is actually a 1974 Dodge B-300 Minnie Winnie Winnebago Class C. Bolt does not give up easily but Tony's mind-operated forces hamper them in their red-and-white Hughes 369HS helicopter, which flies and lands upside down. It's great fun but also edgy, which was one reason the British director John Hough was hired – he'd made his name in cult horror films such as the ultra-creepy *The Legend Of Hell House*. (Walt Disney Productions)

A parochial sheriff in a Georgia town, Reed Morgan (Max Baer Jr) might be smirking but he's casually warning brothers Chris and Wayne Dixon (real-life actor brothers Alan and Jesse Vint) that their kind of teenage thrill-seekers are not welcome in these parts, and nor is their hitchhiker companion Jenny (Cheryl Waters). So they'd better get their car fixed – it has a broken fuel pump that the garage is about to repair – and ship out of 'his town'. They might seem belligerent but they take his advice in *Macon County Line* from 1974. Once they get going again in the second-hand 1949 Chrysler Town & Country convertible, though, they're heading straight into trouble that will bring them back into deadly conflict with Morgan. (American International Pictures/EMI Film Distributors Ltd)

Macon County Line was a small independent film costing $225,000 to make that caught filmgoers' imagination and earned $10m. Although it was presented as some kind of true story it was entirely the fictional work of its star Max Baer Jr and its director Richard Compton. It's a story set in 1954 in the American Deep South, of carefree kicks before joining the military, that takes a dark and lethal turn after their car conks out. The Town & Country was always a distinctive car with its 'half-timbered' look more usually associated with contemporary station wagons. For the 1949 model year a mere 993 examples were built, and their rarity today means pristine examples can fetch more than £100,000 apiece. (American International Pictures/EMI Film Distributors Ltd)

It's likely that if you're watching *Beginning Of The End* then it's because you love creaky sci-fi involving giant locusts, or you're a sucker for so-terrible-it's-brilliant schlock Americana. You might not be expecting much in the way of rare cars, but then this highly desirable 1955 Chrysler New Yorker convertible pops up, driven by agricultural scientist Dr Ed Wainwright (Peter Graves) – the man who'd used radiation techniques to grow gigantic vegetables that lead to the correspondingly enormous insect plague that descends on Chicago, each bug the size of a bus. Here he is in a clinch with investigative journalist Audrey Aimes (Peggy Castle). The Chrysler might be convincing as a superb two-tone period piece but the special effects and none-too-convincing acting would be risible; that is, if the overall kitsch value of this super-low-budget 1957 movie were not so high today. Wainwright saves the day by luring the flying horrors to Lake Michigan, where the cold temperatures kill them off in the nick of time. (AB-PT/Republic Pictures Corporation)

Here, the car actually is 'the beautiful American' of the title in this 1961 French slapstick comedy. Widely mistaken for other large US-built convertibles of the period, in the main Cadillacs, it is in fact a 1959 Oldsmobile 98 convertible in gleaming white. It's highly distinctive in being one of very few production cars to feature no less than six headlights. Marcel Perrignon (Robert Dhery) is a simple-minded worker in a French factory who spots the car for sale at a ridiculously low price in a newspaper advert, and thinks he's found the bargain of the century. The flashy convertible, however, is being sold by the wife of the man's boss, who is furious that her husband has been having an affair and is determined his mistress won't get her hands on the man's prized Olds. Subsequently the car brings nothing but trouble to Perrignon and his wife (Colette Brosset), manifested in the comedy gold of epic traffic jams and car washes with the power roof down. *La Belle Americaine* was released in 1961 and, although very overlooked, is a classic of its belly-laughing genre. One of the funniest jokes throughout the film is of the temperamental factory production line, whimsically making metal rods. (Continental Distributing Inc)

The sight today of Peter Sellers 'browned-up' as a socially clumsy Indian actor, using racial stereotypes straight out of his *Goon Show* days, is a little unedifying. Nonetheless, *The Party* from 1968 is a cult comedy classic, and the only non-*Pink Panther* movie that teamed Sellers up with director Blake Edwards. This scene is typical of the surrealism that brims over on-screen – the moment when a baby elephant is brought to the Hollywood dinner party in the film's title. It arrives in the back of a Lincoln Continental convertible, evidently a very strong vehicle in that its frame can cope with its signature 'clap-door' arrangement (the rear ones rear-hinged) *and* the shifting bulk of a large mammal. Sellers' Dr Bakshi earlier turns up at the wheel of a 1930s Morgan three-wheeler. (Mirisch Corporation/United Artists)

There's little to match the 1960s Mercedes-Benz SL 'pagoda-roof' roadster for 1960s glamour and sophistication, and so the car is a perfect partner for the legendary Joan Collins in the 1970 sex farce *Up In The Cellar*. As Pat Camber, she is wife to the politically ambitious president of the Silver Range College, Maurice Camber (Larry Hagman). After a computer error leads to a young poet (Wes Stern) losing his scholarship, Maurice foils his suicide attempt. Rather than be grateful, though, the student reasons the president has still 'killed' him, philosophically — and proceeds to take his revenge by seducing Mrs Camber, their daughter, and also the college head's mistress. (American International Pictures)

The whole film industry was trying to spoof the James Bond super-spy formula in the 1960s, and *Kiss The Girls And Make Them Die* was Dino de Laurentiis's Italian-American attempt in 1966. The light-hearted comedy was based on the plan by a wealthy megalomaniac to sterilise humanity — apart from his stock of beautiful women — using a satellite, and the efforts of an intrepid CIA agent (Mike Connors, later of the *Mannix* TV show) to stop him. He works with an upper-crust English MI6 agent (Dorothy Provine), and the homage to *Thunderbirds* is completed by Terry-Thomas as her Parker-style chauffeur. Here he is in a scene shot with Provine and the Rolls-Royce Silver Wraith touring limousine, with bodywork by Park Ward, a car stuffed with sci-fi gadgetry to defy its traditional, two-tone elegance. (Dino de Laurentiis Cinematografica/Columbia Pictures)

This Mercedes-Benz 190SL gets a small but impactful part in the Merton Park Studios' B-movie thriller *Solo For Sparrow*, 1962. Here it is with Mr & Mrs Reynolds (Anthony Newlands and Nadja Regin, a Serbian actress who did a lot of work in England in the 1960s) in a scene from the film, the real focus of which is Inspector Sparrow (Glyn Houston) and his determination to crack a baffling but deadly robbery, in his off-duty time. One of the fifty different second features the studio made under the 'Edgar Wallace Mysteries' banner, it's choc-full of familiar British actorly faces, most significant of which is a callow Michael Caine as doomed Irish crook Mooney. (Anglo Amalgamated Film Distributors)

Marcello Mastroianni pulls up at the villa gates in his yellow Fiat 124 Spider, responding to a call from Faye Dunaway. She's an American fashion designer in the final throes of terminal cancer, although he doesn't know that – yet. The film is *A Place For Lovers*, directed in 1968 by Vittorio Di Seca as an emotional, Italian-French co-produced drama. Dunaway has met him briefly before but decides he's the man for a final fling after seeing Mastroianni on TV – he's a racing driver with a keen interest in designing plastic airbags to save lives in car accidents. In real life this echoed Jackie Stewart, who led a high-profile campaign against the Formula 1 authorities and race teams to radically improve safety for drivers in top-level racing. (Compagnia Cinematografica Chempion/Les Films Concordia/Metro-Goldwyn-Mayer)

When it comes to big, flashy-looking American sedans, Cadillacs have tended to dominate on the silver screen, so it made a pleasant change to encounter this 1971 Lincoln Continental in *The New Centurions*. It was a 1972 crime drama in which Roy Fehler (Stacy Keach, right) is a wannabe lawyer who joins the Los Angeles Police Department as an interim job. Unfortunately for both his studies and his family, Fehler gets to really like the work, but when his veteran patrolman partner retires his life spirals out of control. In this well-lit night scene, he's just pulled over a call girl (Bea Thompkins) driving the Lincoln, but when she speeds off with Fehler hanging on to the open window he's going to get one hell of a ride. (Columbia Pictures Industries)

The Quiet American was the first feature film to be made in Vietnam, shot in 1957 and based on Graham Greene's novel. Set five years earlier, it follows an American economist (Audie Murphy) caught up in the dangerous struggle between the French colonial rulers and determined Communist insurgents. All his good intentions are undermined when he starts a romance with the Vietnamese girlfriend of a vengeful English newspaper reporter. Greene was reportedly none too pleased that his anti-war message was brushed aside in this film adaptation by Joseph Manciewicz, and there were all sorts of problems filming in Ho Chi Minh City. However, little of this is obvious on screen. In this ambitious setting outside the Continental Palace Hotel on Dong Khoi Street (Greene had stayed there himself), the devastation of a bomb attack was recreated with the help of several old cars reflecting the foreign empires involved. A late 1940s Panhard Dyna in the foreground is being burnt to a cinder, while just visible behind that are the tails of a late 1930 Oldsmobile and a 1947 Ford Super Deluxe. And right at the back is a Citroën 'Traction Avant'. (Figaro Inc/United Artists)

In a modern-day (1957) Western, the townsfolk of Spurline don't want no trouble. Most of them rely on the Golden Empire cattle ranch run by Virgil Renchler (Orson Welles) for their livelihoods, and when a Mexican ranch-hand is beaten to death by one of his violent employees, they fear ruin if the crime is exposed. Step in newly elected sheriff Ben Sadler (Ray Chandler), who decides he must go against overwhelming local opinion and get to the bottom of the brutal murder; indeed, here is some of the fierce local opposition taking up arms in *Man In The Shadow*, crouching around, on the right, a 1946 Ford Super De Luxe station wagon, and a 1956 Dodge Custom Royal. When Renchler's pretty young daughter decides she's on the side of justice with Sadler, things start to change, but not before the sheriff has been dragged through town tied to the back of a truck – something that simply hardens his resolve to enforce the law in the correct way, and win back everybody's respect. (Universal International Pictures)

The Rank Organisation was keen to stress the realism in its 1963 release *80,000 Suspects*, which was written, produced and directed by the prolific Val Guest, and based on Elleston Trevor's book *Pillars Of Midnight*. It's set in the city of Bath in Somerset where a dangerously infectious disease has broken out. Local doctors and their wives are caught up in the panic-stricken human drama. In this wintry scene, captured by stills photographer John Jay, people coming in from outlying districts are being vaccinated in an effort to contain the epidemic. All the vehicles have been carefully curated by Guest for their authenticity. On the right is an Austin FX3-based ambulance in the livery of the Bath Division of the Red Cross; in the middle is a Bristol Lodekka double-decker used as a mobile surgery – being built in nearby Bristol, these buses were a common sight throughout the West Country; and on the left is a Wolseley 6/99 police squad car so entirely typical of the period. (Rank Organisation)

The stranglehold on the early police-car market held by Wolseley is hard to fathom, but there was no doubt that, in the 1948 Wolseley Six-Eighty, the police had one of the most responsive and powerful saloon cars as both a patrol and a pursuit vehicle that could be bought at an affordable price. The cars were favourites with forces up and down the country, most especially with London's 52-division Metropolitan Police, and the relationship between law enforcers and manufacturer carried on with the replacement Wolseley Six-Ninety. All of which meant that selecting a car for police dramas was a no-brainer; this Six-Ninety appeared in *Attempt To Kill* in 1961,

one of many efficient and broadly enjoyable B-movies produced at Merton Park Studios in suburban Surrey. Like many, it was touted as an 'Edgar Wallace Mystery', a format familiar to cinemagoers between 1960 and '65, but for the USA the films were repackaged for TV under the 'Edgar Wallace Mystery Theater' banner. *Attempt To Kill* concerned a wealthy businessman who fires one of his employees, and then becomes the target of an attempted murder. Here Detective Inspector Minter (Derek Parr) and his Sergeant Bennett (Clifford Earl) are on the case on location near the River Thames in Berkshire. (Merton Park Studios/Anglo-Amalgamated Film Distributors)

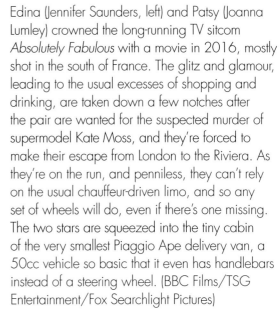

Edina (Jennifer Saunders, left) and Patsy (Joanna Lumley) crowned the long-running TV sitcom *Absolutely Fabulous* with a movie in 2016, mostly shot in the south of France. The glitz and glamour, leading to the usual excesses of shopping and drinking, are taken down a few notches after the pair are wanted for the suspected murder of supermodel Kate Moss, and they're forced to make their escape from London to the Riviera. As they're on the run, and penniless, they can't rely on the usual chauffeur-driven limo, and so any set of wheels will do, even if there's one missing. The two stars are squeezed into the tiny cabin of the very smallest Piaggio Ape delivery van, a 50cc vehicle so basic that it even has handlebars instead of a steering wheel. (BBC Films/TSG Entertainment/Fox Searchlight Pictures)

The Piaggio Ape provides a white-knuckle ride as it careers down a French coastal hillside for Eddy and Pats, as the police try and apprehend them, in a scene that involved careful planning and expert stunt-driving of the wobbly fish-delivery van. It ends its run in an infinity pool but, as is obvious in this shot from the set complete with elaborate camera rig, the stars had to get more than their feet wet for the plunging finale. The battered Ape (Italian for bee) went on show afterwards at the National Motor Museum, Beaulieu, in its 'On-Screen Cars' display. The comedy also starred Julia Sawalha, Jane Horrocks, Kathy Burke, Lulu, Kate Moss of course, and June Whitfield in her final film role. (BBC Films/TSG Entertainment/Fox Searchlight Pictures)

The producers of the James Bond films tied up a big deal with Ford for *Die Another Day* in 2002. It saw 007 (Pierce Brosnan) at the wheel of a brand-new Aston Martin once again, the British marque being at that time part of Ford's Premier Automotive Group division. The chosen car was the V12 Vanquish, Aston's latest creation and notable for being the final new model from the company's venerable Newport Pagnell factory, where less than 1,500 examples were almost entirely hand built. Rocket launchers and machine guns were fitted, naturally. (Eon Productions/Ford)

From another part of Ford's Premier Automotive Group, Jaguar, came the pursuit car for Bond's enemy Zao in *Die Another Day*. It was an XKR convertible, painted the same lustrous green as the short-lived Jaguar Formula 1 team that was contesting the World Championship at the time. The car featured a boot-mounted missile launcher, and this thrilling chase was filmed on location at a frozen-over lagoon at Jökulsárlón, Iceland. (Eon Productions/Ford)

For the rough treatment that the star cars would receive during shooting of *Die Another Day*, standard-issue road specification models, rapid though the cars already were, would not be robust enough. So all of the four Aston Martin V12 Vanquishes and four Jaguar XKRs were actually perfect lookalikes built on four-wheel-drive drivetrains, based on the Ford Explorer sport-utility vehicle. (Eon Productions/Ford)

Behind-the-scenes glimpses revealing how the Bond magic is created are rarely released, but thanks to Ford's major involvement in *Die Another Day* via its ownership of Aston Martin the manufacturer was allowed to issue some unusual images of close-up filming. Here shots are being taken of the V12 Vanquish in icy conditions that would be seamlessly integrated into the final cut. (Eon Productions/Ford)

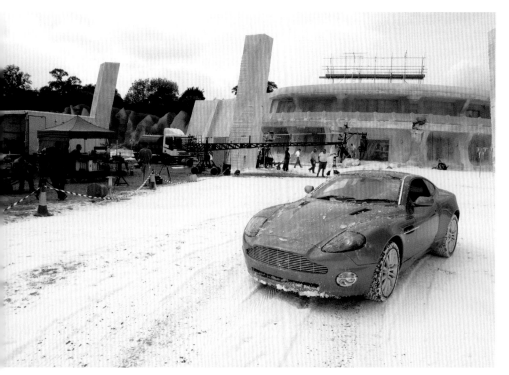

Another on-set photo at the Pinewood Studios backlot which gives an idea of the craft that goes into a Bond film. The Aston Martin V12 Vanquish is being filmed sliding around on simulated snow in the Buckinghamshire countryside while the crew carry on as if it's the most normal situation in the world. For a major production like this, *Die Another Day*, the relationship between carmaker and filmmaker is often symbiotic; a limitless supply of cars, and technical support, is needed for whatever might happen during the shooting schedule, in exchange for products benefiting from the honour of sharing screen time with Britain's most high-profile fictional character. (Eon Productions/Ford)

Completing Ford's extensive involvement in *Die Another Day* in 2002 was this coral-pink Ford Thunderbird for Halle Berry's character of Jinx. This was the car that had a wider commercial tie-in, because in 2003 Ford offered a limited-edition run of 700 examples of the Thunderbird – sold principally in the USA – in an identical colour with a white interior, special twenty-one-spoke chrome wheels, and discreet 007 emblems. (Eon Productions/Ford)

It was a truly wondrous coup for the Rootes Group company to have its Sunbeam Alpine sports car chosen for Alfred Hitchcock's classic 1955 thriller *To Catch A Thief*, to star alongside the suave Cary Grant and the beautiful Grace Kelly. Nonetheless, it was also quite a commitment because identical left-hand drive cars had to be supplied for both location filming on the French Riviera and studio sequences back in Hollywood for reasons of seamless continuity. Here the sheeny, metallic blue Alpine is indeed in a studio-shot scene as retired jewel thief John Robie (Grant) and the American socialite Frances Stevens (Kelly) captivated by his charisma get intimate over a picnic. (Paramount Pictures)

To Catch A Thief was shot by Hitchcock in glorious colour using the latest widescreen VistaVision process, best to catch the brilliant light of the south of France to bedazzle people at the pictures in dark and rainy towns around the world. This shot overlooking the famous rocky coastline captures the glamour reflected by the rare and desirable Sunbeam, with its sleek tapered tail, concealed hood, and ivory steering wheel and dashboard controls. Still, the heavy steering with no power assistance might have been a chore for Grace Kelly at low speeds. This image from a period lobby card contains an obvious error; the black-and-white still photo has been hand-coloured, with a vivid red used instead of the film car's blue to tempt punters to the upcoming presentation. (Paramount Pictures)

Remaking a TV classic that was such a dearly held part of so many childhoods was always going to be a tall order. And the biggest change between the *Thunderbirds* series of 1965–66 and the movie in 2004 was the replacement of puppet characters with real people. On that score, Sophia Myles as Lady Penelope and Ron Cook as her shifty chauffeur Parker shown here won praise for the much-loved characters created by Gerry and Sylvia Anderson. Far more controversial was modern-day tampering with

other aspects of the show for the big screen. The producers failed to reach agreement with BMW, owner of Rolls-Royce Motor Cars, to be able to use anything other, maybe, than a standard Rolls-Royce – and at that time this would have meant the new Phantom – in place of the original six-wheeled car with its FAB 1 registration number. Instead, this six-wheeler was provided by Ford and shared many styling similarities with its recently relaunched Thunderbird production car. (Ford Motor Co/Working Title/Universal)

The new FAB 1 in *Thunderbirds* was able, on-screen, to transform itself into a jet-powered aircraft, and a further divergence from the original was the fact this huge car was now a two-seater, rather than having a single seat up-front for Parker and a wide bench seat in the back for Lady Penelope and any travelling companions. The car was designed in-house at Ford of Europe; it was part of a huge product-placement deal that saw many other Ford vehicles, from the Ka city car to the F-150 pick-up, featured in the movie – an aspect that diehard fans decried. Gerry Anderson himself also disliked the new treatment (but no longer owned the rights) and in the animosity he was even denied a 'created by' credit at the end. With little goodwill, it wasn't a box-office hit. Dedicated fans still had the two *Thunderbirds* cinema films from the 1960s to console themselves with, although curiously neither of those were successes either. (Ford Motor Co/Working Title/Universal)

Rolls-Royce is one of a tiny handful of carmakers to have had its name used in the title of a major film, and in *The Yellow Rolls-Royce* the car really is the central focus, as the Terence Rattigan screenplay explores three stories of people who all owned the same limousine at different times. The first part of the saga revolves around the original owner The Marquess of Frinton (Rex Harrison) who buys it new for his wife only to discover she uses its spacious cabin for her adulterous liaisons. Later on, having covered more than 20,000 miles, the car rocks up in Genoa, Italy, owned by American gangster Paolo Maltese (George C Scott) shown here. (Metro-Goldwyn-Mayer)

Shirley MacLaine plays Maltese's feckless fiancée Mae Jenkins, shown here with her tresses intermingled with the car's Spirit of Ecstasy radiator mascot. *The Yellow Rolls-Royce* was filmed on location but also at MGM's studios in Elstree, Borehamwood, UK. It was there that the production team oversaw the transformation of the Rolls-Royce Phantom II they acquired for the central role. Built in 1932 on chassis number 9JS and carrying an imposing sedanca-de-ville body by London coachbuilder Barker & Co. (catalogued body number 6424), the original blue paintwork was covered up in a reputed twenty coats of bright yellow paint, with contrasting black to bonnet, roof and mudguards. With its worldwide exposure in the film, this Phantom would naturally become highly sought after, and was most recently in the possession of Rolls collector Neal Kirkham of Saratoga, California, USA. (Metro-Goldwyn-Mayer)

When the movie shifts into its third phase, the garish Roller is in a garage in Trieste in 1941, and bought by a wealthy American widow (Ingrid Bergman). Although she's intended to tour Europe in the car, she meets freedom fighter Davich (Omar Sharif) and gets caught up in a dangerous Nazi-busting adventure that sees the car used to storm the border into Yugoslavia. Here they are among the cadre on a winding mountain road crossing into the country, with the Phantom taking the sort of pounding for which it was

definitely not intended. This scene is the reason the car has sometimes been confused with the yellow-and-black Rolls-Royce driven by henchman Oddjob in the 1964 James Bond film *Goldfinger*. This is partly because the same location was used for the high-octane chase between Bond's Aston Martin DB5 and the white Ford Mustang of Tilly Masterson (Tania Mallett). Oddjob's car, though, despite being superficially similar and also carrying Barker sedanca bodywork, was a later 1937 Phantom III model. (Metro-Goldwyn-Mayer)

A spread of imaginary cars have been cooked up between Hollywood film designers and the automotive industry, heavily skewed towards futuristic adventures. This one is the 2003 model year Mercedes-Benz E500, only morphed into a 'strike cruiser vehicle' for Agents J and K to use for pursuing alien spaceships in *Men In Black II* in 2002. You see it here much as you would on screen, only shrunken to a toy model along with a complementary 3.5in-high evocation of Agent J (Will Smith) as sold in Toys R Us at the time. (Daimler-Benz AG)

This is the RSQ that Audi designed in 2004 for the sci-fi film *I, Robot* in a highly professional act of paid-for product placement. Created by senior Audi designer Julian Honig, the RSQ was supposed to represent the sort of technologically adventurous car you'd find on the mean streets of Chicago in 2035. To implant Audi's contemporary image into cinemagoers' minds, it did look a bit like the TT coupe, but the film's director Alex Proyas insisted on the radical move of fitting castor-like spheres instead of conventional wheels. (Audi UK)

This imaginary supercar from Lexus, known as the 2054 to give an idea of its vintage, was the first of the several major tie-ups with carmakers in the early twenty-first century. Lexus worked with Steven Spielberg on its design for his film of Philip K. Dick's novel *Minority Report* in 2002, and star Tom Cruise is seen at the wheel in several key scenes. The master director was already a Lexus owner himself, and the Toyota/Lexus design studio in California came up with the sleek fuel-cell-powered vehicle with lots if his input. However, the Japanese manufacturer also paid a reputed $5m for tie-in marketing rights to associate it to the movie. (Lexus)

In one of the biggest movie car fleets of all time, Land Rover built thirty-one of these twenty-second-century urban vehicles for the 1995 big-screen outing of comic-book hero *Judge Dredd*, starring Sylvester Stallone. They were constructed at the Land Rover specialist Dunsfold Collection's garage in Surrey and delivered to Pinewood Studios in 1994. The jagged exterior design was the work of Rover designer David Woodhouse. Only this one was fully trimmed and operable (they used second-hand Land Rover 101 army chassis, picked for their height), the others all being hollow shells slipped over Land Rover chassis and used as props to represent taxis in a forbidding and futuristic Mega-City One. After filming, half of them reverted to normal 101 specification while the rest were sold to eager Land Rover collectors. (Land Rover)

Mercedes-Benz didn't have to design a jungle-friendly four-wheel-drive off-roader for Steven Spielberg's sequel to dinosaur fantasy *Jurassic Park* in 1997. It already had one in the new luxury M-Class. But for *The Lost World* tie-up the two ML320s supplied had considerable alterations to make them up to the job of exploring the Isla Soma. For one thing, they both had custom-made trailers, but the cars – named AAV Santana and AAV Fontana – were equipped with hefty front bull bars, a frontal tow hitch, winch, fog lights, rear tail-light guards and camouflage paintwork. Santana featured a cut-out rear compartment and exterior jerry cans while Fontana, shown here, had a bubble window roof, bonnet panniers and mirror-mounted searchlights. They both get pushed over cliffs in run-ins with T-Rexs. (Daimler-Benz AG)

Classic car collectors today will likely feast their eyes on this pristine original example of a 1970s Range Rover two-door in its sought-after, period-perfect sage green paintwork with tan interior – now worth a small fortune. But this lobby card image of 'Emanuelle' in *Black Emanuelle* is meant to entice punters to the showing of this 1975 soft-core erotic film, which was rushed out to exploit the worldwide phenomenon of the film *Emmanuelle* released the year before. A second 'm' was omitted from the title to sidestep any copyright issues.

Despite her skimpy outfit (although the handbag looks pretty substantial), Mae Jordan was supposed to be an investigative photo-journalist whose assignments were apt to have an erotic element. Shot in Kenya by an Italian crew, the actress with the Emanuelle name was Laura Gemser, a model the director had reportedly spotted on a travel-agency poster. However, in the flimsiest possible nod to political correctness, she was supposed to represent 'a strong and independent woman'… (Flaminia Produzioni Cinematografiche/Columbia-Warner Distributors)

This demure and seemly image of Dutch actress Sylvia Kristel is not how most of the massive worldwide cinema audience remember her from the highly successful soft-core adult movies she made in the 1970s. There were seven of them in total, starting with *Emmanuelle* in 1974, which caused as much indignation as approval, but nevertheless helped take the genre mainstream for the first time, in most territories heavily censored and flagged up with warnings on its erotic content; the French-made production was the first X-rated film ever released in the USA by Columbia Pictures, and an estimated 300 million cinema tickets for it were sold worldwide. But, before any of that happened, Sylvia entered the Miss Europe TV contest in 1973 aged 20, and won it. Part of the prize was the keys to this brand new, £6,000 Mercedes-Benz 350SL. (Mercedes-Benz United Kingdom)

For carmakers, hiring in the services of a glamorous film star to be seen with their products is a certain way to get attention; and for the performers, it might just mean the gift of a free motor, or perhaps free use of one for a year. In the many tie-ups over the years, this is one of the least-known. Swiss actress Ursula Andress – famous for her white bikini and diving knife on her hip as she steps out of the Caribbean in *Dr No*, the first James Bond film – is here adding her denim-clad allure to the Seat 133 in around 1975. The little 133 doesn't look too exciting, but it's significant as the first Seat that was more than a licence-built Fiat (it was, though, based on the rear-engined 850), and a tentative step to the Spanish car marque establishing its own identity. (Seat UK)

Left: The right car can be an extension of the red-carpet arrival at film premieres, especially when one of the coolest stars steps out of it and into the flashbulb frenzy. Here is Hollywood A-lister Samuel L. Jackson and the XJR 100 provided by Jaguar for the London opening of his film *The 51st State* in 2001. Just 100 of these limited editions were built. He's sporting a rather fine kilt. The film was a British-Canadian co-production also starring Robert Carlyle, Emily Mortimer, Meat Loaf and Ricky Tomlinson in an action-comedy set in Liverpool. (Jaguar Cars)

Below: Michael Caine posing for a photo with one of the very last of the original Minis in 2000, shortly before production of the car came to a halt after 5.3 million examples had been built over forty-one years. When he and the Mini made *The Italian Job* in 1969, he didn't have a licence and couldn't drive (like so many actors). Recently Caine admitted that he got his first practice behind the wheel on that movie, because so much filming was done in closed-off, non-public highway locations. This car's bonnet was hand-signed by 'Charlie Croker' in 2000 before being sold in an ITV charity auction. (Rover Group)

A selection of essential cars from the James Bond canon. In *Casino Royale* in 2006 Aston Martin supplied this pewter-coloured DBS V12; it was sparingly equipped with gadgets, running to just a secret compartment for Bond's Walther PPK handgun, and a medical emergency kit with direct links to MI6 headquarters. (Aston Martin Lagonda)

In *Quantum Of Solace*, released in 2008, another example of the Aston Martin DBS V12 gets a severe bashing at the beginning of the film in Siena, Italy. (Aston Martin Lagonda)

The Aston Martin DB10 marked the first time in twenty-four movies that a model from the British sports-car company had been custom-made for a role with 007. Ten examples were built for use in *Spectre* starring Daniel Craig as James Bond in 2015, eight for actual filming purposes and two for promotional duties. The car was unveiled by producer Barbara Broccoli and director Sam Mendes in 2014 to kick off the advance promotion of the movie; Mendes was also intimately involved in the car's looks and functional capability with Aston's chief designer Marek Reichmann. Although the outer shape remained unique to the DB10 (and none was ever sold to the public), the car acted as a subtle preview to the all-new V8 Vantage model that made its debut in 2017. (Aston Martin Lagonda)

Above: Lotus Esprits have appeared in two James Bond films, here in *The Spy Who Loved Me* of 1977 and also *For Your Eyes Only* of 1981. In the former, the white S1 performed dual roles as road car and submarine with anti-aircraft missiles. Much of the fast driving in the movie was performed by Roger Becker, a Lotus engineer who travelled with the car on location to Sardinia. (Group Lotus/Eon Productions)

Right: The BMW 750iL that James Bond (Pierce Brosnan) toys with to destruction in *Tomorrow Never Dies* from 1997 is handed over by Q (Desmond Llewellyn), complete with Ericsson mobile phone from which the car can be remote controlled. (BMW GB)

Count Louis Zborowski was a racing aristocrat of the 1920s whose spectacular, aeroplane-engined racing cars thrilled the watching crowds – as the 27-litre engines rarely revved at more than 1,500rpm at venues like the Brooklands track in Weybridge, Surrey, they gained the nickname of 'Chitty Chitty Bang Bang' for their thudding soundtrack. James Bond writer Ian Fleming loved them, and based his 1964 children's book on a similarly awe-inspiring car with magical powers. Three years later, Albert 'Cubby' Broccoli, producer of the 007 movies, turned Fleming's fairy tale into a film with the help of author Roald Dahl, which was first screened in December 1968. Here the car is axle-deep in the sea on location on the French Riviera with, left to right, Caractacus Potts (Dick Van Dyke), Truly Scrumptious (Sally Ann Howes), Jemima Potts (Heather Ripley) and Jeremy Pots (Adrian Hall). (United Artists)

The cinematic Chitty Chitty Bang Bang was no aero-engined monster. Its impressive early 1920s form was the creation of production designer Ken Adam, and half a dozen examples were built by the Alan Mann Racing team in Weybridge. Five of the cars were used for studio, film set, flying sequences and special-effects work, as shown here in a rare glimpse of the film set at Pinewood Studios. Interesting to see that the crew have plastered a large warning on a windscreen so the cast won't hurt themselves during close-ups. The one working car featured a Ford V6 3-litre engine and automatic transmission, more usually found in a Zodiac or Capri – although the sound of a veteran Hispano Suiza was dubbed on to the film soundtrack for 'authenticity'. It had to be robust enough to withstand mistreatment during filming but still exude a hand-made coach-built character. The wheels, for example, looked like wood but were actually painted cast alloy with tyres specially moulded by Goodyear to give modern standards of road grip, and the dashboard was adapted from a First World War fighter plane. Broccoli kept the roadgoing car at Pinewood but, when no sequel seemed likely, he sold it to a professional clown Pierre Picton in 1972, complete with GEN 11 number plate, with the proviso that Broccoli had first refusal if he got sick of it. That was probably the reason Picton turned down an offer for the car from pop star Michael Jackson in 1991, reputedly for over $10m. In 2011, with Broccoli dead, the car sold for $805,000 at a California auction, passing into the custody of New Zealand film director Sir Peter Jackson. (Author's collection)

This one-off car, the Silver Volt, has a small place in automotive history in that when it was launched in 1979 it was the world's first modern-day petrol-electric hybrid. The prototype was built by the Electric Auto Corporation, and was designed to appeal to wealthy 'early adopters' similar to the people who bought the first Teslas almost exactly thirty years later. Based on a much-modified Buick Century, it had a huge battery pack feeding a 50kW electric motor and was supplemented – as in a modern hybrid – by a small petrol engine, a 150cc rotary from a microlight aircraft.

This generated power for the car's electrical equipment, but was also an on-board range extender, allowing the driver to limp home at 15mph should stored battery power run out. The Silver Volt's first brush with film royalty came when actors Jack Lemmon and Lloyd Bridges had examples on loan, and Lemmon even drove his to the Academy Awards. Teething problems meant the car never went into series production, but it did make a bizarre return to the public gaze capturing a scene in the 2003 teen secret agent film *Agent Cody Banks*. (Author's collection)

Mike Myers as Austin Powers had already poked fun at the Jaguar E-type in two previous films, calling it the 'Shaguar' and generally making it a part of the ridiculous, over-sexed persona for his 1960s British playboy/secret agent spoof character. No one would have been surprised if Jaguar had disdained anything to do with it, but such was the worldwide liking for Powers' infectious humour that, instead, Jaguar joined in for the 2002 film *Austin Powers In Goldmember*, providing a new Shaguar in the shape of a Jaguar XK8 convertible wrapped in the usual Union Jack flag. Its special features included bulletproof glass and an ejector seat button for Austin to spring himself out of the car when things got tricky. It could also be remote-controlled, from his wristwatch. The film was another giant success… and Jaguar's US monthly sales subsequently doubled. Although there are several replicas, the original film car is in a private collection in the USA. (Jaguar Cars)

These two Mini Coopers were employed in the 1998 big screen reboot of 1960s TV classic *The Avengers*, and provide some of the car interest along with the Jaguar E-type driven by Emma Peel (Uma Thurman) and the Bentley 4.5-litre of John Steed (Ralph Fiennes). There's more, too, as the film has cameos from a Vanden Plas 3-litre, Wolseley 6/110, and a Wales & Edwards milk float. (Rover Group)

What might have been: the film *Run* was announced at the 2004 Cannes Film Festival and was all set to star Rick Yune fresh from his appearance in *Die Another Day* and Simon Webbe, of pop band Blue. Also announced for its big-screen debut was the 175mph MG X-Power SV, the new high-performance supercar from Britain's MG Rover Group; it was supposed to be part of the custom-car-inspired plot of illegal, late-night racing and nitrous-oxide injected engines. The $10m action adventure set in Britain's urban underworld, however, met the fate of hundreds of movies over the years that have been heralded but not fulfilled. Filming, set for July 2004, never began. And within a year, MG Rover had gone bust and the SV was no more anyway. But al least posterity has left us this launch photo. (MG Rover Group)

US motor sport writer Brock Yates was so frustrated at speed restrictions placed on American drivers that he staged the Gumball Rally in the early 1970s. This informal road race ran from New York to Los Angeles, the first of which Yates won driving a Ferrari 365GTB/4 Daytona in 1971 in a record thirty-six hours. The maverick spirit in this two-fingers-to-authority adventure was picked up for several later movie comedies of which *Cannonball* in 1976 was the first. It was named for Erwin 'Cannonball' Baker, a famous coast-to-coast record-setter and the lead character was Coy 'Cannonball' Buckman (David Carradine), a paroled prisoner who contests the fictional transcontinental road race from California to New York in a red Pontiac Firebird Trans-Am. Among his competitors were high-minded European professional racer Wolfe Messer (James Keach)

in a yellow De Tomaso Pantera, beach bums Jim and Maryann Crandell (Robert Carradine and Belinda Balaski) in a silver Chevrolet Corvette, and Beutell Morris (Stanley Clay) in a black Lincoln Continental. There's plenty of double-cross and subterfuge, but most of all loads of high-performance driving and stunts, including an impressive jump over the gap in a part-finished bridge. This scene of piled-up carnage occurs soon after a doppelganger Firebird is slipped over, setting off a chain of impacts and explosions that makes a great spectacle but makes you wonder why drivers would keep charging straight into the inferno. A dozen or more cars including the 1964 Ford Thunderbird seen bottom left were wasted, and even David Carradine apparently expressed concern at the scene of wanton wreckage. (New World Pictures)

Quentin Tarantino regularly cites *Dirty Mary Crazy Larry* as one of his favourite movies, and it's a fixture in many top-ten car-chase lists. Larry Rayder (Peter Fonda) is a NASCAR driver with skill and potential but no finance, and so with his mechanic Deke (Adam Roarke) he decides to pull a heist on a supermarket cash office to get funds. His one-night stand Mary Coombs (Susan George) proves keener than Larry first realised and they make their initial getaway in this 1966 Chevrolet Impala, which makes a daring leap over a slowly rising river bridge. Ultimately, though, they need more horsepower, and a 1969 Dodge Charger R/T makes the ideal getaway car, especially as it has a police scanner and two-way radio. At the end of the piece, it seems the 'speed kills' message rules. For filming, two Impalas and

three Chargers were used, and the Dodge muscle car is noteworthy for its 'Citron Yella' paintjob, which can appear alternately more yellow or more lime green depending on the age and quality of the print version of this high-octane classic you're watching. The crew added the non-standard black side stripe. Six second-hand Dodge Polara police cars were hammered to pieces during production. The ending is decisive and shocking. As this was a low-budget film, a crack team of mechanics were needed to repair and maintain the precious cars while filming progressed, with continuity suffering very slightly as a result, but the 1974 movie was a huge hit, winning mostly acclaim for the cast and British director John Hough. (Academy Pictures Corporation/Twentieth Century-Fox Film Corporation)

Even as far back as 1991, genuine Porsche 356 Speedsters were much too valuable to be risked in the hands of moviemakers. So although it looks as though Michael J. Fox swerved to avoid a cow, careered over a ditch and smashed one into a picket fence in *Doc Hollywood*, the stunt team actually availed themselves of a reasonably convincing plastic replica. In fact, they worked their way through five or six of these VW-Beetle-based lookalikes, some for interior shots only, but a real 356 (a scrap coupe with its roof missing) was used for the final car-crash meltdown. One of the replicas is on display today at the Star Cars Museum in Gatlinburg, Tennessee, USA. Here, Fox as Dr Benjamin Stone is seen with the mess he's made, shortly before paying for it by community service. The car is finally facelifted but his plans to work in California as a plastic surgeon get diverted... (Warner Brothers)

Super-successful 1980s TV comedians Mel Smith and Griff Rhys-Jones made their big-screen debut in *Morons From Outer Space* in 1986, under the reluctant direction of Mike Hodges – he only agreed to helm this screwball comedy-sci-fi, written by the two former *Not The Nine O'Clock News* performers, if Thorn EMI promised to film his script *Mid-Atlantic*… which it did, although in the end the pledge was never honoured after the firm was bought by Cannon Group later that year. The creative collaboration itself was none too happy either, and the film got panned, although subsequently it's been re-evaluated as quite a funny satire on celebrity, packed with jokey references to other sci-fi movies. The story is about a spaceship full of dimwit aliens who crash-land on Earth by accident. One scene that definitely impresses is when their ramshackle craft touches down on the M1 just outside London. Cars such as this Jaguar XJ6 and Hillman Avenger are scattered in all directions, and there's impressive night-time action photography on motorway sections that the producers somehow managed to get access to. (Thorn EMI Screen Entertainment)

This rare Ford Zodiac MkIV estate is rocked backwards and forwards by a desperate mob in a cinematic tale of survival in the face of global panic: *No Blade Of Grass*. Although the film was released in 1970, it's notable that the car has been given a registration number for 1972/3, indicating that the vision of food panic triggered by environmental and deadly-virus apocalypse wasn't seen by the director-producer – Hollywood actor Cornel Wilde – as very far off. The family fleeing London, in a cast headed by the Brit Nigel Davenport and American actress Jean Wallace, do break free of the rabble when police fire in the air, and they head for what they hope is safety in Northumberland in both this Zodiac and a Ford Capri MkI. For a film with eco-concerns at its core, it still seems to be something of a typical violent actioner. (Metro-Goldwyn-Mayer)

The lyrics of Bobbie Gentry's 1967 hit country song 'Ode to Billie Joe' inspired the 1976 film of almost the same name, after the songwriter admitted to an original typo. Billy Joe McAllister himself is a teenager confused and tormented over his sexuality in 1950s Mississippi. He's anxious to woo his childhood sweetheart Bobbie Lee (Glynnis O'Connor) but traumatised by a drunken encounter with his boss. The Tallahatchie Bridge mentioned in the song plays a central part in the story, such as here where the O'Connors' family farm pickup, a beige 1948 Ford F-Series, on its way to market loaded with eggs and milk, is caught in a frightening, smoke-inducing shoving match with a Chevrolet pickup of exactly the same vintage, belonging to three drunken yokels from Alabama. The damaged truck is almost pushed into the river below, which is a teetering metaphor for tragic events that occur later. Director Max Baer Jnr used a bridge on County Road 512 as it crosses the Yazoo Rover at Sidon, Mississippi; this ageing structure was replaced by a modern concrete span in 1987, with plaques at either end to commemorate the filming, which produced an enormous cinema hit when *Ode To Billy Joe* was released. (Warner Brothers)

A RASTAR PRODUCTION

SMOKEY and the BANDIT

A Universal Film Distributed by Cinema International Corporation

The roof has just been torn off this 1977 Pontiac Le Mans, and it's landed on top of an Oldsmobile, in 'Smokey's' frenzied efforts to stop 'The Bandit' in his beer-smuggling tracks. In the comedy road movie *Smokey And The Bandit* this is just one part of the destruction trail that made it so popular at cinemas in 1977 that it finished up second only to *Star Wars* in that year's American ratings. In the story Burt Reynolds is The Bandit hired to act as a decoy while truckers sneak a mega-cargo of alcohol across state lines from Texas to Atlanta for an important bash. Jackie Gleason is his nemesis Sheriff Buford T. 'Smokey' Justice, the law-enforcer obliged to abandon his son's wedding

to give chase; that's the unfortunate groom sprawling on the Pontiac's bonnet (actor Mike Henry). Pontiac itself had a major part in the film, supplying four Firebird Trans-Am cars for The Bandit to drive during filming, all of them in black with huge golden eagle emblems across their bonnets. The whole quartet was just about finished off in the boisterous process. The cars were in fact 1976 cars upgraded to 1977 external appearance. This was to take into account the long period between the start of shooting and the release date. The characters' names, by the way, are their CB radio call signs. (Rastar/Universal/Cinema International Corporation)

Circumstances have not allowed me to ever secure a still from *Fear Is The Key* that depicts the truly spectacular car chase early on in the piece. However, the expression on the face of passenger Sarah Ruthven (Suzy Kendall) seems to sum up the atmosphere pretty well (silly girl, she's not even wearing a seat belt) as her kidnapper John Talbot (Barry Newman) pilots this 1972 Ford Gran Torino like a man possessed. Actually, the chase through Louisiana almost seems transplanted from another film as the tale, based on the Alastair MacLean novel of the same name, moves on to Talbot's elaborate set-up, diamonds, oil rigs and submarines. (Anglo-EMI Film Distributors/Paramount)

Kyra Sedgwick's role in *Something To Talk About* portrays her as a feisty woman, more than able to handle the heavy, non-power-assisted steering in the classic MGA shown here. Finding a presentable left-hand-drive example of the 1950s two-seater roadster would have been no problem – most of them went to the USA anyway. Emma Rae is sister to the main character Grace (Julia Roberts), a woman who discovers her husband is having an affair in this 1995 comedy-drama. Trouble is, her family, Emma included, are nothing like as sympathetic to her trauma as she might expect. However, Emma Rae does administer a killer kick to the testicles of the cheating brother-in-law, part of a performance that won Sedgwick a Golden Globe award for best actress in a supporting role. (Warner Brothers)

The Austin A55 Cambridge of insurance investigator Stephen Maddox (Alan Bates) has just been run off the remote Spanish road and down a rocky mountainside. Road workers and passing motorists (stepping from their Seat 1400B to assist) are helping to drag him from the wreckage before the car tumbles away to crumpled destruction. The perpetrator of this accident was crooked Rex Black (Laurence Harvey) in a stunning white Lincoln Continental 'clap-door' convertible with his horrified wife (Lee Remick) in the passenger seat. They've roared off towards the border with Gibraltar in a final dash to get away with an insurance scam that saw Black fake his own death in an air crash. Desperate stuff in a sun-kissed location in *The Running Man*, directed by Carol Reed in 1963. The film was in glorious colour but this lobby card image seems to be a black-and-white still that's been carefully hand-coloured; the Seat is brown here but blue in the movie! (Columbia Pictures)

America's attitude towards small cars is well illustrated in this film featuring Dean Martin and Jerry Lewis as two demob pals who join the circus and find themselves with new careers as a pair of clowns. The compact, air-cooled Crosley, introduced in 1949, was a singular attempt to interest US drivers in something small and economical in an era when the typical saloon car was becoming a heavyweight, chrome-dripping behemoth with a V8 engine and 16ft or more of over-styled steel. But it was picked for *3 Ring Circus* in 1955 – shot in the then-new Vistavision and glorious Technicolor – because its diminutive size was something that made most people chuckle or, at worst, shake their heads in pity. The Indiana-based manufacturer had actually closed down three years earlier, dwindling sales caused by antipathy to its products, and a reputation for dodgy reliability. The car in the ring here while Martin and Lewis fool around is a 1949 CD convertible-sedan model that, like all Crosleys, had a sub-1-litre engine. In the closing scenes of the film it's used for a visual gag where an endless stream of people step out of its tiny cabin. (Paramount Pictures)

The late, and not so great, John Z. DeLorean could never have guessed his deadly serious sports car would become such a mainstream movie star. For while the gull-winged wonder from Northern Ireland might have sunk in a steaming bog of scandal, it made the perfect time-travelling transport for Michael J. Fox's Marty McFly character in the wildly popular 1985 film *Back To The Future*. McFly, whose family life is a shambles, befriends scientist 'Doc' Brown (Christopher Lloyd) and discovers his boffin chum has turned a DeLorean DMC-12 into a time machine. Here the Doc is explaining its workings to an enthralled Marty, including its outwardly extending wheels, the flying controls and the in-car fax machine. Although the Doc is killed by terrorists seeking their missing plutonium (the DeLorean's calendar-

defying fuel), Marty uses it to go back to 1955 – only needing to wind it up to 88mph – where he can change the course of history so his family life is a much happier one. Early 1950s Americana naturally abounds – Marty finds Mercurys, Chevrolets, Buicks and De Sotos littering the city streets. Tracking down the Doc in his younger form, and harnessing a lightning bolt, eventually hurtles him back to 1985. The plot may be one of the greatest fantasies ever conceived by special effects wizards in an era before CGI even existed, but the cars in both 1955 and 1985 were real enough. And guess what? The father of Marty McFly's girlfriend Jennifer has a 1984 Eagle wagon, seen briefly but gloriously in *Back To The Future*. (Amblin Entertainment/ Universal City Studios)

Here is your chance to see the talented and elegant Nicole Kidman as a teenage BMX bike fanatic in Australian crime comedy *BMX Bandits*, performing amazing stunts against the sunny backdrop of Sydney Harbour. Nicole did learn a lot about BMX riding, although in the film her place is often taken by an athletic double with a wig on. Even so, Nicole managed to sprain her ankle during shooting. The kids stumble across a box of police radio-band walkie-talkies which they try to sell to raise money so Judy (Kidman) can buy a bike to match the professional machines ridden with such panache by her mates PJ and Goose. The handsets, however, have been stolen by a gang of bank robbers, and they want them back. The plot unfolds with some great riding skills on show, such as this airborne leap over a passing MGB roadster, fully capitalising on the contemporary craze for BMX riding. (Rank Film Distributors)

Dune buggies and 'sand-rails' were often confused because they both relied on recycled Volkswagen air-cooled engines. This is definitely one of the latter; a super-lightweight runabout specifically designed for driving on sand and sand dunes. A dune buggy has fatter 'floatation' tyres and, usually, a glass-fibre body for negotiating more shifting sands, and so you can't see the chassis frame 'rails' as you can here in *Angel Unchained*. Airborne and at the wheel is Don Stroud as retired, chilled-out biker Angel, who joins a hippie commune outside a small town in Phoenix, Arizona. When the local rednecks attack his friends, Angel is ready to defend them, and calls up members of the Nomad Chapter of his old Exiles MC bike gang to excise the menace. Shades of *Easy Rider* in this great, leather-clad period piece directed by Lee Madden with plenty of riding, driving and, indeed, flying. Real bikers were recruited as extras. (American International Pictures)

Not a car, clearly, but a Magirus Deutz single-decker bus, sporting a prominent, stylised capital 'M' on its radiator grille, the centre point of which represents the spire of the minster in Ulm, Germany where the dependable vehicles were built. It's in a scene from the 1950 German film *Gabriela* and, despite any appearances that this still may give, it's not a stunt-filled action movie but a melodrama; a musical about a singing star who retires from performing to spend time with her daughter. She discovers that the young lady much prefers the freedom of life in the ski lodge where she grew up than in the nightclub that's the hub of her mum's world. The title role was taken by Zarah Leander, a German actress controversial for her alleged Nazi sympathies, and this was intended as her comeback. It was number three at the box office in Germany in 1950, but perhaps understandably received an icy reception elsewhere in Europe. (Real-Film GmbH/Banner Pictures)

This dishevelled Jaguar S-type driven by German businessman Schneider (Carl Möhner) has just been prevented from crossing the railway line by a barrier. The car has been specially positioned for this still, though, because in the actual scene you see in *Callan* one side is lifted clean off the road and the oncoming train rams into it remorselessly. The 1974 thriller was a big-screen outing for the character of David Callan, the downbeat Special Investigation Service agent played with such scowling intensity by Edward Woodward in the hugely popular 1960s/70s Thames TV series of the same name. It's modest but compelling. Only Woodward and Russell Hunter, *Callan*'s whining gofer 'Lonely', made the switch to the film two years after the TV show ended. Callan is ordered to kill a target to get his career prospects back on track, but before he does so he wants to know why. A highlight of the plot is Callan's intimidating cat-and-mouse car chase with Schneider. This he does in a white Range Rover with blacked-out windows; several times he takes the car off-road where its four-wheel drive is used to great effect so that he can burst through fences and hedges to unsettle his prey. (Magnum Films/EMI)

People say you should never shut a dog in a car on a hot day, but for the human characters in the edge-of-the-driving-seat 1983 horror film *Cujo* there is something of a reversal. Donna and her young son Tad (Dee Wallace and Danny Pintauro) are trapped and cowering inside the claustrophobic cabin of this 1978 Ford Pinto Runabout and have to cope with the threat of heatstroke and dehydration. They're held terrified hostage by Cujo, a hefty Saint Bernard dog who's been bitten by a bat and gone barking mad. It was based on a Stephen King novel of the same name. It would be a pity to give away any more about this cult suspense classic, but in order to make the dog seem as rabid as possible, its tail had to be strapped down so it wouldn't wag happily during filming. Meanwhile, to get the mutt to appear frantic to smash the windows and get into the car, some of its favourite real-life toys had to be placed inside. (Taft Entertainment/Warner Brothers)

Coming to blows: ultra-competitive racing driver Joe Machin (William Campbell, left) has had about enough of motor-sport journalist Steve Children (Mark Damon) in a tense moment from *The Young Racers*. All admirers of classic Alfa Romeos can only hope that the wing of this pretty Giulietta spider isn't going to sustain a dent in the nasty fracas, as Machin reacts badly to Children's plan to write a book exposing his reckless driving on the Formula 1 track, and his caddish behaviour off it. If you revel in the great days of post-war grand-prix racing then you'll love this film; director Roger Corman took his film unit from race to race around Europe in the 1963 season. Before each race he sent a scout on ahead to identify all the best vantage points, and so the human drama unfolds against a backdrop of real footage from races in Monaco, Rouen in France, Spa in Belgium, Zandvoort in the Netherlands and Aintree in the UK. That's why real racers Jim Clark and Bruce McLaren also put in appearances. (American International Pictures)

Goodbye Pork Pie was filmed in 1979 and released in 1981, whereupon it put New Zealand filmmaking firmly on the map. It also renewed the cinematic stardom of the humble British Leyland Mini more than a decade after *The Italian Job*. Geoff Murphy wrote, produced, directed and even performed some of the driving work in this rebellious road movie filmed along the length of both Kiwi islands. It all begins when a punky teenager steals a wallet and then hires a Mini with the cash and driving licence inside it. It ends after chases, ferry and train rides, and the formation of the 'Blondini Gang' in the inferno shown here, when the Mini is finally stopped in its tracks. Local Mini assembler New Zealand Motor Corporation lent three yellow Minis to Murphy's low-budget production; two were returned relatively unscathed while the third – complete with a big hole in its roof – was used for promotions, and apparently still exists. However, the car blazing away here together with an Austin A60 Cambridge was a 1959 scrapper used as a disposable stand-in. Local thefts of Minis reportedly rose after the film was released… (Brent Walker Film Distributors Ltd)

Blooper time: *Coupe de Ville* has a classic Cadillac as its centrepiece in this 1990 comedy about three squabbling brothers and a tough father who tries to get them to bury the hatchet, just not in each other's heads. However, although there was a Coupe De Ville hardtop in the Cadillac range from 1949 until 1993, the car featured is actually a 1954 Series 62 Convertible, probably chosen as a better, more accessible showcase in which to film the cast. The siblings are asked by their dad to drive the car from Detroit down to Miami as a present for their mother, and here Fred Libner (Alan Arkin) is confronting his sons, left-to-right Marvin (Daniel Stern), Boddy (Patrick Dempsey) and Buddy (Arye Gross) about why they've damaged it en route. (Twentieth Century Fox/Morgan Creek Productions)

Any number of movies have featured the iconic Checker taxi that was once the stalwart of the New York 'yellow cab' fleets. Slightly unusually, *D.C. Cab* features a group of scruffy Checkers operating in Washington for The District of Columbia Cab Co. The world-weary drivers include Samson (Mr T, seen here on the right, before he became world famous in *The A-Team* on TV) who have new hope for the run-down business when recent recruit Albert Hockenberry (Adam Baldwin, left) arrives. After a rare violin is found on the dusty back seat of one of the Checkers, the $10,000 reward money looks set to transform the fortunes of the D.C. Cab Co, but Mrs Hockenberry has other ideas. If you love old Checkers then the parade at the end is a party on the screen. (Universal City Studios)

The early film days of Julie Walters are marked by some long-forgotten roles, and it must be admitted that she gives it her manic best in 1986's *Car Trouble* alongside co-star Ian Charleson. It is a natural for this book, of course, despite the pitifully low budget – much of it is filmed on the short concrete drive of a suburban semi – and single, much-laboured joke at the film's climax. Gerald Spong (Charleson) is an air-traffic controller whose mid-life crisis is addressed in that age-old way – the purchase of a sports car, a red 1965 Jaguar E-type Series II coupé which is the apple of his sad little eye. Jacqueline Spong, now sidelined, finds herself taken with the Jag's weasely salesman Kevin (Vincent Riotta), but once in a clinch together the E-type is going to pay the ultimate price. It's a tawdry comedy, with a fate for the Jaguar that's difficult watching for lovers of Britain's greatest ever classic sports car. (Double Helix Films/Columbia-EMI-Warner)

If you want to see a 1969 Morris 1100 MkII Super stretched to its very fibres and keep on going – defying all the usual accusations that British Leyland cars were unreliable – then you'll love this. But even if you don't, *Clockwise* is a very funny film, one of John Cleese's best, in fact. His Brian Stimpson is a punctuality-obsessed headmaster who needs to get to a conference in Norwich but finds everything is out to thwart him. His best hope is one of his pupils, Laura Wisely (Sharon Maiden), who might be skipping lessons and illegally driving the family 1100 without a licence but at least has the wheels that can get him there – on time. Penelope Wilton (future British 'national treasure') joins the mobile chaos en route as Pat, who just happens to be an ex-girlfriend of Brian's. It's not just the rearview mirror that comes adrift; the Morris loses a front wing too, and here Pat is distraught as Brian gives his orders from the back seat. Slightly disappointingly, a Porsche 911 partly saves the day. (Thorn EMI Screen Entertainment)

A bit too gritty for a comedy, a touch too screwball as an action film, *Downtown* actually does a good job at combining both. It's also a buddy move in that two Philadelphia cops have to face the city's criminals together. In fact, there's not much friendship at first because Officer Alex Kearney (Anthony Edwards, here on the left) is a policeman from a quiet suburb foisted upon understandably hostile Dennis Curren (Forest Whittaker) and his tough, city-centre patch. Here they are sitting on an upturned 1986 Plymouth Gran Fury patrol car, typical of the cheap and dated contemporary sedan used by forces across the US. The striking image was also used for the movie's poster. Curren's unmarked '86 Gran Fury does a large portion of the stunt work, picking up plenty of scars en route. (CBS Fox Video)

When an old Jewish lady has to give up driving, and so her independence, her son sorts her out with a driver, which in 1950s Atlanta, Georgia, means a black man. Stubborn and prejudiced, Miss Daisy (Jessica Tandy) gives her employee the very cold shoulder but the African-American Hoke Coleburn (Morgan Freeman) with his patience and gentle manners eventually wins her round. Miss Daisy's car is a new, scarlet 1949 Hudson Commodore, and inside its cosy cabin their resistance to one another gradually melts away and their close relationship builds. Hoke, however, will not be patronised, and sticks to his dignified stance to the nth degree. *Driving Miss Daisy*, released in 1989 and based on a stage play of the same name, also starred Dan Ackroyd as Boolie, Daisy's decent son. As the story moves through some twenty years, the Hudson shown here gives way to a 1965 Cadillac Calais and then a 1970 Fleetwood Sixty Special. It's moving and stays with you. (The Zanuck Company/Warner Brothers)

This book lacks the space to overly recount the plot of *McQ*, the 1974 crime film in which a 66-year-old John Wayne plays a houseboat-dwelling cop investigating drugs and murder cases. Here is the Hollywood colossus pointing a gun at a suspected killer at the end of one of the film's two excellent set-piece car chases. He's just finished chasing a 1969 Chevrolet Step-van with bakery livery around the freeways and shortcuts of Seattle, all wonderfully captured in great locations by director John Sturges (there is, apparently, a city tour even today that can take you to all the interesting pinch-points) and done with deep reverence for Steve McQueen's *Bullitt*. Wayne's car is this 1973 Pontiac Firebird Trans Am 455, the Super Duty edition of which a mere 255 were built that year, and even more desirable thanks to its lustrous Brewster green paintwork. At the end of the movie comes the second famous pursuit, filmed on the beach of the Quinault Indian Reservation in Washington. Wayne in a 1969 Plymouth Belvedere is harried through sand and sea by both a 1971 Cadillac Sedan De Ville and a '74 Chevrolet Impala; the sequence is notable because stunt driver Hal Needham made the first ever use of a black powder cannon charge to flip a car over without using ramps. However, during practice beforehand on studio backlots, an accidental overcharging of the detonator almost killed him, and colleague Gary McLarty performed the deed for the film. Wayne took on a not dissimilar cop role for his London-based police film *Brannigan* a year later. (Batjac & Levy-Gardner/Warner Brothers)

This still from *Badlands* hardly does justice to the stunning photography in the 1973 teen murder flick, the acclaimed directorial debut of Terrence Malick. It does, though, capture something of the bleak nihilism of the piece, which was based on the real-life murder spree committed by 20-year-old Charles Starkweather and his 14-year-old girlfriend Caril Ann Fugate in 1958. In the movie, Holly (Sissy Spacek) is 15 and her beau is 25-year-old dustman Kit Carruthers (Martin Sheen), with a penchant for the rebellious James Dean look that's a guaranteed turn-on for

any young girl. After Kit shoots Holly's heartless dad dead, the pair go on the run across the badlands of Dakota. Being set in the late 1950s, they come across a black '59 Cadillac Series 62 sedan when robbing a mansion, and set off in it as the ideal getaway from the trail of shootings in their wake. They could have taken his red Rolls-Royce Silver Cloud, but the Caddy it has to be. Here they have reached Montana while fleeing towards the Canadian border, but their luck – like their relationship – is quickly running down. (Warner Brothers)

Fans of the TV series *The Dukes Of Hazzard* will instantly recognise John Schneider in his very first leading film role in *Eddie Macon's Run*, released in 1983 while he was taking a break from television work. Car fans may have trouble spotting the car because it's not the usual cheapo Ford or Dodge customarily used in a Hollywood chase. It's a Mercedes-Benz 300SD, the luxury diesel-powered S-Class much pushed by the manufacturer in the US market. Although Schneider as the eponymous Eddie Macon is poking out of the shattered rear window, the glass has been broken by a gunshot from

Kirk Douglas as prisoner chaperone Marzack, who is in hot pursuit (far more predictably in his 1976 Dodge Coronet). Macon has jumped prison in a cattle truck and the Merc is owned by rich girl Jilly Buck (Lee Purcell) who turns from hostage to getaway driver as she tries to help Eddie cross Laredo to rendezvous with his wife. The film was shot six years after the James McLendon novel of the same name was published, with its characters derived from his own family; as McLendon died in 1982 he never saw his story come to life on the big screen. (Universal City Studios Inc)

Duel is such a haunting thriller/horror movie that even today drivers recall it with foreboding whenever they see an articulated lorry getting too close in the rear-view mirror. This 1971 TV movie, and indeed the extended 1972 cinema release which featured additional, newly shot scenes, marked the film debut of no less a giant of cinema than Steven Spielberg. It relays the story, brilliantly suspenseful, of travelling salesman David Mann (Dennis Weaver) who is terrorised by the driver of a sinister Peterbilt petrol tanker over a long and unnerving road trip. Mann's car was a 1971 Plymouth Valiant, a humdrum, low-priced American sedan chosen for its red colour, to show up well in the desert-road filming locations, and with mediocre power so that it would be increasingly vulnerable to the thunderous truck on its tail. (Universal Pictures)

A stern Eli Wallach steps from the leather-lined cabin of a 1976 Cadillac Fleetwood 75 limousine – he's Sal Hayman, an ex-spy recruited by the FBI to help solve the murder of a chemist. His solution is to hire a former mafia hitman, James Coburn's Jerry Fanon, to nail the blighter. The 1979 thriller *Firepower* was filmed across the US and the Caribbean by Michael Winner, who also wrote and produced this international star-laden extravaganza with Sophia Loren, Coburn and OJ Simpson topping the bill. There are guns, explosions, planes and cars – including a white Hillman Hunter – aplenty, and what with the glossy locations the convoluted plot becomes fairly hard work to follow. All the finance was British but, for Sir Lew Grade (who grudgingly let shooting go ahead even after the promised Charles Bronson declined the chance to star), the budget splashed on-screen was not rewarded with critical success. (Associated Film Distribution)

Subtle it ain't: *Death Wish 3* is the epitome of the violent action thriller, with a head-spinning tally of bullets, bodies and car crashes as Charles Bronson, then 64, reprised his vigilante role, and his partnership with director Michael Winner. His character Paul Kersey is this time seeking to eliminate a street gang that's terrorising old people, but even the star condemned the film for its excessive violence. These days, *Death Wish 3* has a cult following because its mindlessly explosive action is so over the top, and many films since this 1985 actioner – which topped the US box office – are now far more sadistic. This scene of a 1977 Plymouth Volare smashing into a 1974 Chevrolet Impala coupé before bursting into flames on its roof occupies just a few moments of screen time in the film, which was shot recognisably in New York and also, to save production costs, on several cunningly disguised London locations. (Golan-Globus/Cannon Productions NV)

Forza G was retitled *Winged Devils* for its very limited theatrical release in the UK and USA. It's an Italian-made adventure-comedy set in the world of aerobatic display pilots where their in-flight antics are matched by their adventures at ground level. An Italian pilot is desperate to join the Frecce Tricolori team, and resorts to buzzing his colonel in this Piper PA-25 Pawnee light aircraft to get his attention. Colonel Moschin (Mico Cundari) is driving his Fiat 124 Spider, immaculately attired with driving gloves, and finally relents. Car vs plane is great fun, and there's plenty more flying excitement shot against cloudless Italian skies. (Vides Cinematografica/United Artists Corporation)

It was a struggle to find any information on *Downbeat* before discovering this title was used only for Britain, and that this is a spectacular scene from the often lampooned, but still entertaining, 1958 US film *Daddy-O*. That hefty 1949 Ford Custom sedan, nicknamed the 'shoebox' for its chunky, slab-sided lines that made it a milestone in post-war American car styling, lands with shocking force after its jump from a truck-loading ramp. The cop, meanwhile, is cowering behind his 1957 Plymouth Plaza patrol car, with its prominent rear fins. The dated 'hip' dialogue and the fact the lead character Phil (Dick Contino) has an alter ego as cheesy singer Daddy-O make the film a fun slice

of kitsch. But it's compulsive viewing for car fanatics as Phil, a part-time truck driver, is challenged to a drag race by mystery blonde Jana (Sandra Giles), their competing 'hot rods' being a 1956 Triumph TR3 and a '56 Ford Thunderbird. After he loses his licence, Phil lands a new job warbling on a nightclub stage, only to find he'll be obliged to take the Ford's wheel for illegal delivery jobs. Classic American B-movie fare for the necking teen audience of the times. First released in a double bill with *Roadracers* (see page 101), this was the first ever film with a score by John Williams. (Imperial Productions/ Anglo Amalgamated Film Distributors Ltd)

If you can stomach all the subsequent sex and violence (the British Board of Film Censors called *Death Weekend* aka *The House By The Lake* 'an appalling orgy of destruction…' but still passed it largely uncut as an X-rated movie in 1976) then this film offers a tense chase between the 1967 Chevrolet Camaro on the left and the 1970 Chevrolet Corvette on the right. Shot in the remote backwoods of Canada, Harry (Chuck Shamata) is a rich dentist with seedy designs on Diane (Brenda Vaccara), a former model. He lets her drive his Corvette to his mansion in the country, but after she runs the Camaro containing a gang of drunken yobs off the road revenge is in the air. The damaged Camaro is retrieved from a creek bed and hell is unleashed when the hoodlums eventually track the couple down. The story was inspired by a real-life report of a Canadian dentist whose home was invaded by thugs after he upset them, and also a nasty road-rage incident experienced by writer-director William Fruet. (Brent Walker Film Distributors Ltd)

As it was filmed in both contemporary Rome and San Francisco, there is plenty of car spotting to be done in *Street People*, an Italian-financed crime comedy released in 1976 and now largely forgotten apart from the odd casting of Roger Moore as Ulysse, an Anglo-Italian mafia fixer. Starring with him, and shown here, was Stacy Keach as his friend Charlie Hanson, a racing driver who's going to help Ulysse get to the bottom of a large religious cross sent from Sicily to the US with $1m of heroin crammed inside it; vague shades of *The French Connection* there. What you see here is Hanson stepping from the smoking remains of a 1975 Chevrolet Monte Carlo, a car he has just test-driven in a comic-book destruction derby lasting five minutes, during which parts detach themselves from the car in a way that could only have been rigged up by a special-effects team anxious to make the sequence look as madcap as possible. (American International Pictures)

Dwayne Hickman as hunky Todd Armstrong is looking dazed and confused after wrecking his MG TD. He's just driven around the corner in the background and been unable to stop the car in time to avoid hitting a gorgeous woman crossing the road. The ramifications were not what he expected because the lady strolled away unhurt and smiling while her elegant frame stoved in the front of his sports car. The 1965 movie was *Dr Goldfoot And The Bikini Machine*, a big-budget parody of contemporary spy films, with Vincent Price as the crazed genius Dr Goldfoot whose steely robot women seduce and rob wealthy tycoons, with Armstrong out to thwart him. It surely had some influence on the *Austin Powers* series. We don't actually see the accident up-close; the crew must have smacked the MG into a few lampposts so it could be revealed as damaged after the scenes were intercut. What a waste. An elaborate chase sequence at the end involves a runaway San Francisco tram as part of the great footage shot around that city. (American International Pictures)

Wild Ones On Wheels was an extremely low-budget 1962 crime thriller very much enlivened by this quartet of open-topped classics. Nearest the camera is an MGA, next is an Austin-Healey 100/6, and then a Triumph TR3. These British roadsters belong to the villains, thugs who've got wind of a $250,000 cash treasure trove that recently released prisoner Duke Walker (Sydney Mason) has stashed away. Him and his big mouth; now they're chasing him and his girlfriend Hazel (Francine York) driving a Willys Jeep CJ5 into the Californian desert to get their hands on it. The sports-car casting (they're all foreign-built, so no grumbles from the Detroit industry giants about unflattering associations) makes a change from the usual motorbike gang, for sure, and there's plenty of great shots of the cars in convoy on the sun-drenched highway. Directed by Rudolph Cusumano with some pretty laughable dialogue, it's enjoyable pulp fiction in celluloid form. (Emerson Film Enterprises)

Taken by stills photographer Rico Torres, this is Esai Morales as the rebellious Jesus 'Chucho' Sanchez in the 1995 American drama *My Family*, the saga of an immigrant Mexican family living in California over three generations, from the 1920s to the 1980s. In the narrative, then, this is mid-period late 1950s, with son Chucho – one of six – strutting his stuff in his pride and joy, a 1940 Mercury coupé that's been lowered, customised and painted in a lustrous metallic red. You'll enjoy the Mambo routine where Chucho leads the local kids in a dance all around the eye-catching car. (New Line Cinema)

Silent Movie was a lovingly crafted comedy in which three producers decide they'll make a film that revives the genre from before the 'Talkies' arrived forty years earlier. The film's soundtrack consists of music, sound effects and just one spoken word, 'Non!' uttered with brilliant invention by mime artist Marcel Marceau. Mel Brooks conceived, co-wrote and directed it in 1976; the story is about the attempts to make a slapstick movie in the Charlie Chaplin tradition to save a bankrupt studio, and to recruit contemporary stars to appear in it. Brooks bought a brand-new, yellow-painted Morgan 4/4 that features throughout, and here he is at the wheel with comedy sidekicks Marty Feldman (centre) and Dom Deluise. The car was sold afterwards to Dick Gastill before it joined the collection of Morgan fanatic Al Gebhard. (Twentieth Century Fox/Rank)

Here's a wacky road movie with a difference. Rather than tracking the customary American misfits, this odyssey follows the fortunes of a hopeless Siberian rock-and-roll band as they seek fame and fortune across the USA. In *Leningrad Cowboys Go America* from 1989, the band travels from New York to their first major gig in Mexico in an appropriately ramshackle 1975 Cadillac Fleetwood 75 stretch limousine, which is a good match for their outrageous, foot-high quiffs and crazy winkle-picker shoes. For most of the journey a frozen member of the band is transported in a box on the roof, along with a stock of beer, and at one point the Caddy's engine gets stolen. Almost the whole cast was from Finland, where they were members of the real band The Leningrad Cowboys. American director Jim Jarmusch has a small role as the car dealer who sells them the Cadillac. (Orion Pictures Corp)

Stories about the making of *It's A Mad, Mad, Mad, Mad World* – which had more guest stars than any other film and was tremendously successful on its 1963 opening – could fill a book on its own. It's also packed with cars, as five motorists set out to snag a stash of cash buried by a hitchhiking ex-convict. Another driver, Otto Meyer (Phil Silvers), gets caught up in this epic chase, and this great on-set image shows Silvers waterlogged in the Kern River with his 1948 Ford Super De Luxe convertible well out of the running. (United Artists)

The Italian-built, Chevrolet-powered Iso Grifo – with its stunningly attractive styling by famed design house Bertone – has risen hugely in value since this still was taken in 1975. The highly desirable car has just crash-landed after launching itself off a small mountain of roadworks gravel outside Rome as its occupants Tracy 'Mahogany' Chambers (Diana Ross) and Sean McAvoy (Anthony Perkins) had a hands-off-the-wheel ride of terror while arguing. The windscreen has detached itself and will shortly shatter on the ground while every frontal panel of Bertone's artfully shaped nose on the Iso gets dented or creased. The very successful 1975 film *Mahogany* has Ross as a struggling Chicago fashion student who finds global success with an Italian-based designer; her former partner Berry Gordy, founder of Motown Records, made his directorial debut with the rags-to-riches saga, and the soundtrack naturally featured Ross's unique voice. Fiat gets a credit at the end for supplying the 'automobiles'. Could it be they found an Iso for the producers, rather than see a Ferrari (Fiat owned the marque) trashed…? (Paramount Pictures)

This is a decidedly dodgy Rolls-Royce Silver Cloud II. It had a big part in the 1972 crime drama *Hickey & Boggs* starring Bill Cosby (left) and Robert Culp, who was also in the chair for his first and only feature-film directorship. The car was bought for the film on a tight budget of less than $6,000 by stunt driver Bill Hickman. This bargain sticker perhaps explains why the radiator grille doesn't really fit the bonnet; this denotes it as a Bentley S-type that's been upgraded for a quick buck. It really was peppered with bullets for this shoot-out scene between the two inept private eyes and mobsters on the LA beach, and the producers repaired the damage afterwards. Soon after it was finished, the 'Rolls' was impounded by well-informed law enforcers, who took it apart again. According to Culp, they found 2lb of pure heroin hidden inside the sills in a real-life version of *The French Connection*. (United Artists)

The idea of an evil genius, based in London, plotting to take over the world with 50,000 radar-controlled, uranium-powered robots seems ever less far-fetched these days, although it must have been a shocker when *Old Mother Riley Meets The Vampire* was released in 1952. US horror stalwart Bela Lugosi took the sinister role of Von Housen because he needed to earn money to get back home after a London play he'd lined up was cancelled. His star quality made Humber willing to supply a black Pullman that's featured throughout the comedy film, and indeed even gratefully acknowledged in the opening credits. The Old Mother Riley character was a comedy drag act, popular with kids, of Arthur Lucan, who made fourteen films in his slapstick oeuvre. (Rootes Group/Renown Pictures/Columbia Pictures)

No one takes reports of a UFO landing in Britain seriously, but then a tipsy motorist driving his Vanden Plas 4-Litre R knocks down a strange-looking chap on a deserted country road, and takes him to a nearby cottage hospital. The accident victim is actually an alien, and while fellow invaders are hunting for him/it across southern England, a strange force field springs up around the place. It's so impenetrable that even this speeding Morris Oxford MkIV Traveller can't break through. The car appears to crash into mid-air, wrecking itself and sending its driver, an unfortunate advert for wearing seat belts, smashing head first through the windscreen and dying instantly. The plot of *Invasion* sounds preposterous, for sure, but the execution was incredibly skilful considering the minuscule budget involved; the lack of special effects, alien costumes or even much incidental music is compensated for by eerie photography and an unnerving tension that rises throughout this modest British B-movie. There are excellent performances from Edward Judd and Valerie Gearon as tetchy doctors in an effective little film that really stays with you. (Merton Park Studios/Anglo-Amalgamated Film Distributors)

Gangster Joey Rosselini (Adam Baldwin) and his sidekick Rhino (Valentino Cimo) return to their car to find a message from Truman Gates (Patrick Swayze), a cop who is out to nab them for the killing of his brother. The mob war has just notched up a gear in Chicago after Gates hurls one of Rosselini's men through a restaurant window, and now they've come back to their 1988 Lincoln Town Car to find the accompanying message. In earlier scenes set around warring families, the car ends up missing its wheels after being parked in the 'wrong' part of town. *Next Of Kin* was released in 1989. (Warner Bros)

After his triumph in *In The Heat Of The Night,* Sidney Poitier was back in his role of police detective Virgil Tibbs for this sequel entitled *They Call Me MISTER Tibbs* in 1970. Now he's working for the San Francisco Police, he's assigned to the case of a murdered prostitute in which a street preacher with political ambitions is the prime suspect. However, in his investigations, Tibbs has a confrontation with a local villain called Rice Weedon that culminates in the policeman defending himself by shooting Weedon dead in an underground car park. Actor Anthony Zerbe is corpsing brilliantly in this well-lit scene where he has to loll out of the driving seat of his metallic blue 1965 Ford Mustang hardtop. (United Artists)

Peter Sellers was a fast-car fanatic, with an addiction so intense that by 1967 – five years after he'd made *The Wrong Arm Of The Law* – an article in the AA's *Drive* magazine described him as 'the compleat automaniac' and reported he'd owned eighty-five cars, including 'a Jaguar for one day, a Volvo for two, a Rover for three'. His close friend and fellow *Goon Show* comedian Spike Milligan called his obsession 'metal underwear' after he ordered both a Lincoln Continental and a Rolls-Royce Silver Shadow coupe in March 1966. Sellers' appetite for the motoring high life was whetted in April 1959 when his brand-new Bentley S1 Continental was delivered, and he was so protective of the car that he spanked his son Michael for splashing paint on it one day in the garage. Yet it was barely run-in when Sellers decided to buy an ex-Cary Grant Silver Cloud I, and when he tired

of that he advertised it in *The Times* under the heading 'Titled Car Wishes to Dispose of Owner'. By 1963 he'd branched out into real exotica, owning both an Aston DB4 GT Vantage and a Ferrari 250 GTE. Both of these appeared in *The Wrong Arm Of The Law* that year, a crooks caper comedy about police impersonators in the London underworld. This scene is at the climax of the film after Sellers as gang boss 'Pearly' Gates in the Aston has just led the Wolseley 6/90 MkIII police car in the background on a frenzied chase. Tony Crook, former owner of Bristol Cars, held a Sellers chequebook and bought more than two dozen cars for the manic actor. 'Often he would change his mind two minutes later anyway,' he recalled. 'But I never found him nasty or annoying – just incredibly tiring to be around. He never stopped or knew quite what he wanted.' (Romulus/British Lion)

American entrepreneur Preston T. Tucker – the subject of this 1988 rage-against-the-system movie, starring Jeff Bridges – was something between idealist and maverick. He wanted to create a car that was as safe as it was rapid and luxurious. Tucker had been an office boy at Cadillac, a car salesman, and partner in an Indianapolis racing-car business before deciding to revolutionise car design in post-war America. Early ideas in 1945 were for a streamlined coupe with a rear-mounted 9.7-litre air-cooled engine, front and rear seat belts, a padded dashboard, frontal crumple zone, and a windscreen that popped out in a crash. In 1946, Tucker acquired the then largest factory building in the world, a former Chicago aircraft plant, in which to make his car, and then hit the publicity trail. But while he was away his management team reconfigured the car, dropping the seat belts because they felt they implied the car was unsafe, and ditching novel features like its swivelling headlamps, disc brakes and a central driving position. Tucker was livid but he was frozen out, and public goodwill evaporated when US financial regulators alleged serious fraud. He protested innocence – and an industry conspiracy against him – and his name was eventually cleared, but the Tucker Corporation went into liquidation after delivering just fifty-one cars, of which forty-seven survive. Francis Ford Coppola's *Tucker: The Man & His Dream* was a pretty faithful dramatisation of this sorry saga; he worked closely with Tucker's surviving family, while Bridges captured the optimism and frustration brilliantly. It took Coppola an agonising fifteen years to bring the story to the screen, driven by memories of his own father, who was an early investor in Tucker. Along the way his original vision of a musical was dropped for a more conventional biopic format emphasising the importance of a supportive family, and George Lucas came on board. As you might expect for such an obsession, the final film came out at three hours long, which distributors insisted on cutting substantially, meaning some key historic scenes that had been lovingly recreated were lost. Members of the Tucker Automobile Club of America lent twenty-one cars for filming, and a further four plastic replicas were specially made for crash scenes, based on cars as diverse as 1950s Studebakers and 1970s Fords. Stills photographer Ralph Nelson Jr took this image of Bridges in the back of one of the cars used. A few facts were twisted to boost the film's dramatic impact, the main one being the scene showing a production line – Tucker never got that far in reality – while the story is portrayed as a year-long saga whereas the Tucker project unfolded over four. (Lucasfilm/United International Pictures UK)

Morris Minors, hugely popular though they were in real life, don't make for very compelling eye-candy on screen, although the convertible has had a few low-budget appearances because with hood folded it's easy to see cast members in character at the wheel. Here, though, a well-used Minor 1000 was probably chosen because its meek performance was a good match for the personality of indecisive American schoolmistress Anna Vorontosov (Shirley MacLaine). Filmed in New Zealand in 1961, many of the children are Maoris flummoxed at Western teaching methods. The dithering teacher is torn between two men, Jack Hawkins as the primary school inspector William Abercrombie and – here – Laurence Harvey as the exciting but drunkard fellow teacher Paul Lathrope, keen to defrock the worthy spinster. It was all a bit much for Britain's ABC cinema chain, which banned it, resulting in a very limited release. Shirley MacLaine was apparently none too happy with the result, especially as she turned down *Breakfast At Tiffany's* to make it. (Metro-Goldwyn-Mayer)

Warner Brothers' *Pete Kelly's Blues* was set in the 1920s jazz age with spellbinding performances from both Ella Fitzgerald and Peggy Lee. Part musical, part gangster movie, but never wholly either, it's a tale of extortion and divided loyalties. The man in the title is leader of the Pete Kelly Big 7, which performed at a low-rent Kansas City speakeasy. It was a great role for Jack Webb, who produced and directed the film and also created and starred in the *Dragnet* police show on radio and TV.

Here is Webb at the wheel of a Studebaker President seven-seater touring car that can easily accommodate his whole ensemble in its three rows of seats; next to him in the front passenger seat is Joey Firestone (Martin Milner), the drummer who is shot by the mob, and just behind him is a young Lee Marvin as fellow band member Al Gannaway. They're just about to be run off the road by racketeers 'persuading' them they need protection. (Warner Brothers Television Distribution)

If what we see on screen is true in the stock-cars-on-ice racing scenes in *On Her Majesty's Secret Service* then Diana Rigg is a fantastically talented driver. While being chased by Blofeld's henchmen in their 1963 Mercedes-Benz 220S, she leaves the narrow Swiss road and diverts straight into the milieu of a race taking place on an ice rink. This has Minis and Ford Escort MkIs sliding around merrily as Tracy di Vincenzo (Rigg) pushes her Mercury Cougar between them. The Blofeld Merc tries its valiant best to follow suit. All the time James Bond (George Lazenby) chats away in the passenger seat as though they're driving through the Whitehall traffic on the way to an admin meeting at MI6. Although Tracy and James dance their way out of the race in the dented Cougar, the Mercedes 'Fintail' (*Heckflosse*) ends its day here, upside down and with the villains escaping flames. The ice track was specially constructed in 1969 on a disused airfield near Lauterbrunnen village in Bern, Switzerland, sprayed constantly with snow and water as the stunt drivers flailed around. The Corgi advertising hoarding is interesting; the Swansea-based toy car company produced an ice-racing set based on the sequence featuring Tracy's Mercury and two Ford rally cars, now highly sought after. (Eon Productions/United Artists)

Nicky Henson is the leader of a motorcycle gang called The Living Dead as Tom Latham. They have a fine time terrorising innocent citizens in a shopping precinct in *Psychomania*. But they could really run riot if they were immortal, something that Tom achieves by killing himself and then coming back to life thanks to his mother, a medium played by Beryl Reid. Here the gang are putting the frighteners on drivers of a Ford Capri MkI and Ford Transit MkI minibus. Despite the white lines on the tarmac, this was not shot on the public road but at what is almost certainly the Military Vehicles & Engineering Establishment test track at Chertsey, Surrey. Amusingly Henson, a keen biker, recalled eagerly signing up to the film on the basis that it would feature Harley-Davidson 'Hogs' to ride, but when he turned up it was these 'clapped-out' AJS, BSA and Matchless bikes, with eight mechanics toiling valiantly to keep the virtual wrecks running. This 1973 supernatural British horror film is now a certified cult classic. (Benmar Productions/VCL Video)

Hard to imagine comedian Spike Milligan as a leading man, but he did a good job of entertaining cinemagoers in 1962 in *Postman's Knock*. He plays a country postie who receives a promotion that takes him to London. His work rate is phenomenal and he becomes the hero of the hour when he foils a bank raid. Here Spike and his mailbag are getting entangled with an Austin Mini in one of many slapstick routines. It has to be one of the earliest of all Mini appearances at the movies, and the scruffy car itself already looks like it's lived a hard life on the capital's streets; there are also telltale signs of a racy life in the bonnet catches and 'bullet' door mirrors – the sort of sporty modifications later found on customised Mini Coopers. (Metro-Goldwyn-Mayer)

This compound stills image with helpful labels gives an idea of the car-related action variety awaiting cinemagoers in 1984 for the comedy film *Police Academy*. 'Cadets are trained in the most scientific tactics to ensure the safety of the community,' jokes the caption. 'Directing traffic' features obvious mayhem as the pallet truck crushes the Pontiac in its wake. A very tired-looking Triumph Spitfire 1500 is the foil in 'High-speed pursuit' – an old car then, yet indicative of what a relatively common sight small British sports cars still were in the USA. Meanwhile, 'Emergency inspection' and 'Parallel parking' both use an unlucky American Motors Ambassador as the object of mirth. (Ladd Company/Columbia-EMI-Warner Distributors)

Directing traffic

Emergency inspection

High-speed pursuit

Parallel parking

At one of the very lowest points in the British film industry's history, brand new TV station Channel 4 stepped in with some welcome finance to get a few small movies off the ground. 'TV movie' was a slight denigration, although they would air first on Britain's new terrestrial channel, as a few of them did make it onto cinema screens. This one, *Red Monarch*, was made by David Puttnam's Enigma in 1983, and was a witty black comedy on a subject that was usually no laughing matter – the life of brutal Soviet totalitarian Joseph Stalin. The two star performers in this satire are Colin Blakely and David Suchet. Recreating this Russian motorcade scene, captured by renowned film stills and poster photographer David Appleby, must have tested the prop buyers' resources in finding sinister, big, black American cars like Packards as doubles for Stalin's ZIS limousines. (Enigma/Goldcrest/Film4)

If it's the cream of European and American sports-racing cars you crave in period action then *Roadracers* is definitely for you. If you saw this film on release in 1959 – in which the father of a racing driver blames his son for a death on the track, disowns him, and sponsors a rival – then it was probably paired with *Daddy-O* (see page 81) in a horsepower-rich double bill. Among the familiar ACs, Corvettes, Ferraris, Porsches and Jaguars, this car is the most unusual. It was based on a Kurtis 500X two-seater but heavily modified for an aborted assault on the 1957 Mille Miglia road race in Italy by renowned hot-rod pioneer Ak Miller. He renamed the Chrysler Hemi-engined car 'El Caballo II', and it was so powerful that after the film in which it was driven by leading man Joel Lawrence, Miller wound it up to 176mph when running at the Bonneville Salt Flats. (Catalina Productions/Anglo-Amalgamated Film Distributors Ltd)

A romantic comedy set in Italy is bound to include some beautiful locations, and the stunning Amalfi coast provides part of the sun-drenched backdrop to *Only You* from 1994. Here is the cast, left to right, captured by stills photographer Emilio Lari: Giovanni (Joaquim De Almeida), Peter (Robert Downey Jr), Kate (Bonnie Hunt) and Faith (Marisa Tomei).

They're on a drive to Positano on a group quest to find the man Faith thinks might be her soulmate. Audiences wanted and expected a cool car, but it would have to have four seats. Fortunately this Ferrari Mondial convertible – one of the very few open four-seaters with a mid-mounted engine – proved ideal. (Columbia Tri-Star Films UK)

When a man with no legs rolls up on his trolley alongside you in your 1972/3 Cadillac Deville hardtop and shines a torch straight into that leather-lined cockpit then you have a right to look shocked. In the complex and sleazy goings-on in 1975 New York in *Report To The Commissioner*, assistant district attorney Jackson (William Devane) is getting vital information from Vietnam vet Joey Egan (Bob Balaban), a beggar who knows the streets well. The gripping story is from Abby Mann, creator of *Kojak* on TV and so adept at convincing NYPD drama, in this case centring on a female detective undercover to nab a big-time drug-dealer – so well undercover, in fact, that a naïve young colleague goes way too far in his investigations (a complex way to make her assignment appear entirely convincing) to find her. The scene where the dealer, Tony King (Thomas 'Stick' Henderson), skips across moving traffic barefoot and in his underpants lets you see plenty of gas-guzzling Detroit metal rolling through the city grid system is this classic '70s New York cop film. (United Artists Corporation)

When selecting the stills to promote the film, you might have expected the publicists to include the 1965 Mercury Park Lane, in a picturesque state of scruffiness, that features so prominently in *Rafferty And The Gold Dust Twins*. But no. The only car element to be found in the eight-photo set is this dusty 1974 Chevrolet Nova, complete with parking dent. The girl with the gun is Rita 'Frisbee' Sykes (Mackenzie Phillips) at the tense climax of this road movie in which two female drifters take control of the down-at-heel, alcohol-soaked life of a Hollywood driving-test inspector. This is the Rafferty of the 1975 title, played by Alan Arkin, while the other woman is McKinley 'Mac' Beachwood, Sally Kellerman. They all set off on a road trip to Las Vegas in the tatty Mercury, and their adventure twists as they pull scams to pay for fuel and refreshments. Having recently filmed *Slither* (see p.27), Kellerman wasn't keen on another road movie, but agreed because her role was as an aspiring country and western performer, and so she gets plenty of opportunity to demonstrate her singing talents. (Warner Brothers)

A 1957 Chevrolet Bel-Air Sport two-door is at the centre of things in 1975's *Return To Macon County*, which was a sequel to *Macon County Line* of a year earlier. It is, however, another serving of a similar story rather than a continuation, to try and capitalise on the earlier movie's explosive success. The two films were among many at the time to use 'drive-in' scenes as part of their plots revolving around carefree teenage road trips that suddenly turn dark, and innocence senselessly mistaken for delinquency. Bo and Harley (early film roles for the pimply Nick Nolte and Don Johnson respectively) are two young fellas taking their souped-up, customised yellow Chevy across country to California in 1958, to have a pop at the Grand National Championship drag races. In Macon County, Georgia, they get sidetracked into a drag race with local high-school boys in a 1949 Ford V8 Fordor, who are furious at losing – as shown in this scrum – and hound them out of town. It's at that point, now with a troubling female hitchhiker on board, that the local law are determined to put them away at all costs. Two near-identical Chevys were dressed up for filming, and in 2014 one of them was unearthed in a Kentucky garage still bearing the holes that had been drilled in its body for camera mounting brackets. (American International Pictures)

There're some rudimentary but still entertaining special effects in *Visit To A Small Planet* where the ever-hyper Jerry Lewis – as Kreton, an alien from planet X-47 – uses his special powers to launch a car above the turnpike to avoid a traffic jam. He's also pretty good at levitating a traffic cop, and pulling his trousers down. The 1960 comedy was based on the Gore Vidal play of the same name, and the car cast was an almost new 1959 Plymouth Belvedere convertible. Here is Lewis (centre) with his adoptive suburban family, actors Joan Blackman and Earl Holliman. (Paramount Pictures Corporation)

Young lawyer Fred Palmer (Robert Clarke) gets a shot in the arm of the very worst kind from dangerous 'one-armed bandit' slot machine operator Monk Walter (Roy Barcroft, a character actor who specialised in villains), which is what can happen when you get mixed up – however innocently – with the Mob, and a bit of romance keeps you ensnared. *Street Bandits* was a tough, American-made crime-drama B-movie released in 1951, and for period car spotters there was plenty to note on the street of the title, including here the 1948 Cadillac Fleetwood 75 stretch limo that's just pulled up, and the 1949 Nash Ambassador behind it and to the right. (Republic Pictures International Inc/GN Pictures)

105

Trial By Combat, or *A Dirty Knight's Work* under its US release title, is a rather forgotten action comedy from 1976 about British toffs turned vigilantes. Donald Pleasence heads the Knights Of Avalon who mete out justice in their idiosyncratic, mediaeval way, challenging criminals they believe guilty to fierce jousting contests rather than just straightforward execution. However, they're on the back foot once a retired Scotland Yard detective, played by John Mills, sets out to investigate.

Feisty Barbara Shelley and thug Brian Glover get too close for comfort in their disparate efforts to thwart Avalon, and are chased down and challenged by thundering knights on horseback in this Mini Clubman estate with period 'nudge bar' on the front. Despite some nifty driving across fields and through woodland – super camerawork capturing the best on-screen Mini manoeuvres since *The Italian Job* – the white Clubman gets utterly pulverised and ends the chase in a pond. (Warner Bros Inc)

The Siata 850 Spring is an obscure car at the best of times, a retro-look two-seater a bit like an Italian Morgan. Made from 1967 until 1970, the Fiat 850 engine was at the back but Italian designer Enrico Fumia created an MG-like radiator grille, free-standing headlights and separate front mudguards to give it the looks of a traditional 1940s sports car in the MG TD mould. With small numbers made, few people would recognise the car but for its near-constant exposure in *Trafic*, Jacques Tati's 1971 French-Italian movie. It was the last cinematic outing for his whimsical life-observer Monsieur Hulot. In it he actually plays a car designer anxious to get his Altra camping car conversion of a Renault 4 to the Amsterdam motor show. He is aided, and sometimes frustrated, by the company's chic PR girl (model-turned-sometime-actress Maria Kimberly) driving the Siata in convoy. Many daft moments include her opening the car's wheel cover, behind which is a fashionable wide-brimmed hat instead of a spare. As a gentle satire on 1960s European motoring culture, there's nothing else quite like *Trafic*. (Les Films Corona/Films Rodo)

The Dirty Weekend, in its Italian release title *Mordi E Fuggi* (Hit & Run), and in its Spanish release as in this still, *Sabado Inesperado* (Unexpected Saturday), is a 1973 Italian comedy. A long pantomime-like car chase features numerous Alfa Romeo police cars among other period classics, and is used to show the absurdity of a media feeding frenzy. The story is one of a high-level kidnapping; wealthy industrialist Marcello Mastroianni is abducted by a gang of communists led by our own Oliver Reed, when all he wants to do is spend the weekend with his sexy girlfriend. Reed is shown here driving a Mercedes-Benz 250S speeding away from pursuers in a Fiat 238 van. In the process he ploughs through a gaggle of rural priests on bicycles, although the Lord saved any of them from getting anything more than bent handlebars. (Metro-Goldwyn-Mayer)

This little film is about men's attitudes to women, and how little their outlook lets them understand the opposite sex. In *Patti Rocks*, Billy (Chris Mulkey) is a man who got a woman pregnant when working away from home, and needs his friend Eddie (John Jenkins) to come with him as moral support when he has to break the news that he's already married with a family. Much of the first part of the movie is about their drive through the night to Minneapolis in a 1965 Ford Galaxie 500 to Patti's apartment for the big showdown, and the script crackles with the tasteless banter that betrays so much of Billy's thoughts. Stills photographer Joel Warren took this image of the two men inside the classic Galaxie. In the end, though, there are surprises all round, especially as Patti (Karen Landry) wants nothing from Billy except for a photo that she will one day give to their as-yet unborn offspring. It's a comedy which proves, in the words of one reviewer, that 'immature men will always be losers'. (FilmDallas Pictures)

The Rank Organisation's stills photographer George Ward took this on-set portrait of Peter Sellers (right) and Cyril Cusack between takes in *The Waltz Of The Toreadors* in 1957. The veteran car is a 1904 Tony Huber, a short-lived French marque produced by an engine firm that was later folded into Peugeot. This very car has been a much-loved regular on the famous London–Brighton Veteran Car Run right up until the present day. In this film, where Sellers plays the retired General Leo Fitzjohn, who has retired to his mansion in the English countryside to write his memoirs but whose history of womanising is coming back to bite him, Cusack is the local motoring Dr Grogan, who can't offer much succour, especially as Fitzjohn much prefers horses to these newfangled motor cars anyway. Watching Sellers, then in his 30s, as a retired soldier twice his age sounds like it's terrible, but he's actually great at it. (Rank Organisation)

The body lying on the ground is that of rancher Jim Calhoun (James Mitchum, son of Robert) who appears to have just been gunned down by Chucho (Erik Estrada, later of TV's *CHiPs*). The film is *Trackdown*, 1976, in which a young girl decides to leave Montana behind her and head for fame in Hollywood, only to be tricked into sex slavery. Calhoun, her beefy, Stetson-wearing brother, sets off to check she's on the straight and narrow, and discovers how deep in trouble she now is. The mud-spattered pickup, which gets driven all over Los Angeles during the film, is a great choice for Jim. It's a Ford F100 with the Supercab option introduced in 1974, adding a 22in extension to the cab that allowed a rear bench seat to be fitted. It's completely typical of the sort of rugged trucks sold all over rural American for tough agricultural duty – well out of step with most of the LA traffic. (United Artists)

Dustin Hoffmann as you may not have known him before, as a career petty criminal pushed to his limits by a manipulative parole officer who thinks he can trade rehabilitation favours for revelations that grass up other prisoners. The film is *Straight Time* from 1978 and, although Hoffman had a spectacular fall-out with the producers over creative control, and filming ran over budget and over schedule, it garnered great reviews. Hoffman's character Max Dembo has here just thrown away all chances of a peaceful life by grabbing the wheel of the yellow AMC Matador sedan belonging to officer Frank (M. Emmett Walsh). The car careers all over the freeway, threading through traffic and scaling bankings before Dembo handcuffs his nemesis to the steel barriers and pulls his trousers down before speeding off. Great scene in a movie well worth revisiting. (Warner Brothers)

This Boy's Life made a true movie star of Leonardo DiCaprio (18 at the time) as a kid, Toby, struggling to comprehend the violent, abusive nature of his new stepfather. The man seems like a godsend to Toby and his single mother Caroline (Ellen Barkin), offering the stability they crave when the itinerant duo meet him after arriving in Seattle. But Dwight (Robert De Niro) has a dark and dominant side that Toby experiences first-hand when his mask of bonhomie slips. Dwight's pride and joy is this 1955 Buick Special 40 Riviera hardtop in crisp blue-and-white, and things get even worse for the defiant, underage Toby when he takes the car and crashes it. Set in the 1950s, there's an authentic resonance to the story, its mental abuse and control-freakery, because it's based on the real-life memoirs of writer Professor Tobias Wolff. Sentimental it isn't. (Warner Brothers)

Pete Menzies is sitting on the roof of his mother's Bentley MkVI and steering it at the same time as he travels across the outback with his sister Rikky in search of fun and fortune. And if you think that's risky enough for a valuable British classic saloon, you'll squirm in your seat when you see him cut the car in half to turn it into an articulated truck. *Rikky & Pete* was released in 1988, a wacky road movie set in Australia, the siblings being a geologist who wants to be a country & western singer (Rikky, Nina Landis) and a restless inventor (Pete, Stephen Kearney) who wants a receptive outlet for his left-field genius. His father sneered at his invention of a machine to fold newspapers into paper darts to fire into people's front porches (mounted on the back of a Mini Moke), so now he's left suburban Melbourne behind in search of people who like him to think differently. An amusing film for everyone bar Bentley Drivers' Club members. (United Artists Pictures)

This is Valerie St John and James Donnelly in a fine slice of period British cinematic sleaze, *The Wife Swappers*, which was a near-permanent fixture in the less salubrious of Soho's cinemas for years after its release in 1970; these days the film directed by Derek Ford and produced by Stanley Long seems a quaint way to titillate with its faux-documentary investigation into a 'swinging' London, and plentiful nudity. Made on a minuscule budget, there were still enough resources to generate this publicity still of the adventurous couple about to step into their shiny Jaguar MkX for an illicit exchange session. That's also quite a rare car in the background on the right, an Armstrong Siddeley Sapphire. The film's narrator is a brazenly fake psychologist who commands the smut-loving audience through a supposedly serious investigation into very strange married lives through six unconnected stories. Ford's later film was called *Commuter Husbands*, but with precious few interesting traffic jams. Today we have Apple Macs; then it was dirty macs… (Salon Productions/Eagle)

Jolly Grimm (James Coco) shows off the fancy 'ice cream suit' designed by Ralph Lauren for his part in the Merchant-Ivory production of *The Wild Party*. He is also leaning arrogantly on the fender (mudguard to Brits) of the Packard that would have been one of the newest and most impressive of American cars in the film's setting of 1929, and so perfect automotive casting. His on-screen wife Queenie was co-star Raquel Welch. He's an ageing silent-movie star desperate to sell his latest, self-financed film to a Hollywood that's left him behind in the unfolding era of the 'talkies'. The party in question is the event he stages to lure studio heads in to see the material, but it turns into an impromptu orgy. All of which leaves the vulnerable former celeb even angrier than he looks here. (American International Pictures)

This elaborate countenance of an Excalibur Series I – the world's first production 'replicar' – gets only fleeting screen time in this film but was clearly diverting enough to make the final stills selection for *Ride In A Pink Car*, released in 1974. There's a British RAC badge bolted to the radiator grille among other emblems. The plot revolves around the long-delayed return to a small Florida town of Gid Barker (Glenn Corbett, shown here on the left and a fixture on US TV from his long service in series *Route 66*), a Vietnam war veteran. Gid's reception is decidedly frosty, and then his attempts to rebuild his standing are shattered when he accidentally kills the son of a leading citizen. Most of the rest of the film is spent on the run from the local lynch mob, where the reference to the film's title finally makes sense: Gid steals a brand new, bright pink 1974 Plymouth Satellite from a dim-witted tourist. (Clarion Pictures Inc.)

114

Three pint-sized forest-dwellers called Knobby, Rufus and Jasper demonstrating the special effects (strictly pre-CGI) that made the 1967 Disney musical comedy *The Gnome-Mobile* such a hit with the kids of the day. In one of the final films personally overseen by Walt Disney himself, this 1930 Rolls-Royce Phantom II with cream-and-black sedanca-de-ville coachwork by London's Barker & Co. gets star billing. But only after it's renamed the 'Gnome-Mobile' by two kids on a road trip with their grandfather, timber tycoon DJ Mulrooney – who bought the Roller when he made his first million. After meeting the gnomes in a redwood forest, an adventure begins that eventually leads to the trees being saved from logging destruction as precious gnome habitat. The Rolls was loaned by vintage car dealer Sam Bergman for the film, but afterwards it was bought by a close friend of Walt Disney's, Donald S. Gilmore, and it became one of the founding exhibits of his Gilmore Car Museum in Hickory Corners, Michigan. It was displayed with a giant-sized rear seat that Disney had specially made to cope with filming the gnome characters at real-life size. (Walt Disney Productions/Buena Vista Distribution Co. Inc.)

Unquestionably the car highlight here is a fancily co-ordinated road race through French mountains between Michael Caine in his Alfa Romeo Montreal and Maureen Kerwin in her Porsche 911S Targa, with dust-scattering doughnuts aplenty. Director of photography Douglas Slocombe also shot *The Italian Job*. *The Marseilles Contract*, aka *The Destructors* in the USA is a 1974 thriller in which drug-busting US agent Steve Ventura (Anthony Quinn) is out to get slippery French narcotics baron Jacque Brizzard (James Mason), John Deray (Caine) being picked by Ventura to head

for the Mediterranean port to do the dirty work. In this scene, Ventura has just managed to flee Brizzard's henchmen in the Citroën DS23 by leaping out at this set of Parisian traffic lights and diving into the Metro. One of the thugs is just managing to avoid being flattened by a Mercedes-Benz 200 taxi before a thrilling pursuit given tingling excitement by the Roy Budd score. Classic '70s French cars abound throughout the movie but you'll notice the opening credit reads *Marseille Contract*, which distributors insisted would be easier to understand for the public! (Warner Brothers)

The Gods Must Be Crazy is quite possibly the funniest film ever to feature an early Land Rover in a starring role. It's a delightfully hilarious piece of work anyway, directed in 1980 by South African Jamie Uys, and set in Botswana. One day a Coca-Cola bottle is thrown from a passing aircraft and found by Xi (N!xau), the head of a peaceful bush tribe who exist totally isolated from the modern world. It causes so much trouble that Xi sets off to return it to 'the Gods', and his odyssey eventually finds him in and out of prison for trapping a goat, and then working as a tracker for idiot biologist Andrew Steyn (Marius Weyers). It's Steyn's

c.1956 Land Rover Series I 86in-wheelbase hardtop that then enters the scene, known as 'The Antichrist' for its wayward behaviour due to a near-total lack of brakes. Xi learns to 'drive' it, in some impressive stunt work, and one hilarious sequence sees the Land Rover's winch pulling it up into a tree, during which a lightweight plastic double for the car, laughable in its inaccurate appearance as a prop, is left dangling from a bough. In this still, Steyn is using the Land Rover's number plate to haul in a rock that can stop it rolling away while he opens a gate. (CAT Films/Twentieth Century Fox Film Corp)

A considerable part of *The Fast And The Furious* seems to be filmed in the snug-fitting cockpit of a Jaguar XK120, as it races around the long-gone Pebble Beach race circuit in California. In fact, here we have some XK-on-XK action as the pale two-seater roadster tussles with a darker drop-head coupé in the fictional event – a cross-border contest that is supposed to allow escaped prisoner Frank Webster (John Ireland) to illicitly slip over the border into Mexico so he can get away from a trumped-up murder charge, and then prove his innocence. A ludicrous scenario, of course, but one packed with urgency. The racing scenes, both shot specially for the film and intercut with footage of real-life sports car events, are a treat for all classic-car enthusiasts, as is a scene set at the annual Pebble Beach concours d'elegance car beauty pageant. Webster

initially kidnaps go-girl Connie Adair (Dorothy Malone) and flees with both hostage and her car, but the trucker fugitive is tailed by police almost from the start in this drama produced by the legendary genius of compelling low-budget flicks Roger Corman. It was the second film he produced, in 1955. To save costs, Corman himself stepped in as one of the competing drivers in the race, but apparently got so carried away that he accidentally 'won' it, leading to a retake. Rights to the title, but not the story, were later acquired to be used for another *The Fast And The Furious* film about fast cars in 2001. Look out for brief appearances from a galaxy of classic machinery, from Aston Martins and Allards to Nash-Healeys and Porsches. (Palo Alto Productions/Anglo Amalgamated Film Distributors)

'Cyclops' must surely be the largest roadgoing vehicle ever purpose-built for a feature film – a huge, articulated bus that, thanks to being nuclear-powered, can drive non-stop at 90mph from New York to Denver. More commercial breakthrough than mere public transport, the 110 passengers could enjoy a built-in bowling alley, cocktail lounge with a piano bar, swimming pool, captain's dining room, and a private marble-and-gold bathroom with sunken tub. Here is the designer Kitty Baxter (Stockard Channing) as the vehicle is about to make its much-vaunted maiden voyage in the 1976 comedy drama *The Big Bus*. But before it could even depart the Big Apple, the scientist behind the bus, the driver and his co-driver are all killed in an accident. And

then a bomb scare on-board – courtesy of an evil plot by oil sheikhs to destroy this threat to their oil-financed livelihoods – makes it an unstoppable trip from hell, especially for the more nervous passengers. Not terribly successful on release, it's now a certified cult movie. The bus itself was built to the design of production designer Joel Schiller. It had thirty-two wheels, with an automated tyre-changing system, and a gigantic Cyclops-eye headlight on its sloping frontage. In contemporary reports, it was said that the two parts of the bus were connected on-set but that the rear section still required its own driver, who needed to communicate by radio because once on the move he couldn't see ahead. (Cinema International Corporation)

This is a scene from the Parisian set of the 1959 French-American film *The Happy Road*. It starred twinkle-toed dance legend Gene Kelly, seen here in the hat and tie, and Barbara Laage, who's sitting in the back of the 'jeep'; for the French military vehicle is actually a very rare Delahaye VLR, standing for Véhicule Léger de Reconnaissance – Light Reconnaissance Vehicle. Delahaye sold 4,000 of these four-wheel-drive off-roaders to the French army before the force switched to a French-built version of the Willys Jeep itself, which was cheaper and simpler. The comedy was about pupils at a Swiss private school who break out for some high jinks in France, while the vintage three-wheeler roadster passing casually by is a Darmont Special. (MGM)

wheel. In reflective mood, the Vietnam War vet turned cop turned cross-country delivery driver finds his past catching up with and overtaking him on a high-speed dash, clashing with a freakshow of real and imaginary foes and counterparts en route. Twentieth Century Fox did Chrysler a favour in giving its latest performance machine such exposure, but Loftin rated the car anyway for its speed and robustness, and the Challengers only required heavier-duty shock absorbers to cope with the rigours of filming in Nevada, Colorado and Utah. Still, Newman, who reportedly found them overpowered, put one car in the undergrowth in avoiding a head-on smash with a member of the public when it was loaded up with lightweight

Whenever stunt co-ordinator Carey Loftin rated a car for film work then everyone would know it was well up to the task ahead. After all, with key car work on great films like *Grand Prix*, *Bullitt* and *The French Connection* to his name Loftin know his stuff, and was the natural choice to coach and advise on *Vanishing Point*. He also brought with him Max Balchowsky to prepare and maintain the five Alpine white Dodge Challenger R/T 440 Magnums used for filming this drug-addled odyssey from Denver to San Francisco, with an overtired and tripping Kowalski (Barry Newman) at the

Arriflex II camera gear to record him as he drove. In this still, Kowalski is close to the end of his trip, and the bulldozers are one roadblock he just can't evade. The race sequence between the Challenger and a stripped-out Jaguar E-type sees the British car eventually out-gunned… a little unjust because enthusiasm from British film fans made Fox re-evaluate *Vanishing Point*; despite a very poor initial showing in 1971, a re-release in a double bill with *The French Connection* began its journey to cult status among both petrolheads and director peers who admired the work of director Richard Sarafian. (Twentieth Century Fox)

This incredible photo, taken at the tense climax of Joseph Losey's horror film *The Damned* just after the car has been chased down by a helicopter, has a real, live stunt driver at the wheel of the Jaguar XK120 (chassis number 660638) as it smashes through the side of a road bridge and makes a violent, diagonal plunge into the river below. Obviously, it could never have been the actual Oliver Reed in character as aggressive yobbo King, but the man chosen for the take — which could only be performed once, and occupies less than ten seconds of screen time — must have been anxious that the preparation and calculations all went to plan. You can see the Jaguar's rear wheel-arch spat being torn off as it charges through the railings. The film itself is an unsettling sci-fi story of motorbike gang violence and a secret military plot to conduct radioactivity experiments on unwitting children. Losey was a noted director, working in England (the film was shot on location in Weymouth, and this is Ferry Bridge) after being blacklisted in Hollywood, and a perfectionist. The movie's release was delayed by two years until 1963 because of his refusal to trim seven minutes from the run-time. (Hammer Films/Columbia Pictures)

He had no name, and very little dialogue. Ryan O'Neal took the title role in *The Driver*, financed by Britain's EMI in 1978 during its short-lived period as a Hollywood player. He is known throughout the Los Angeles underworld as *the* person to go to if you want a speedy getaway and the very best chance of not getting caught. Almost immediately after the film opens, the taciturn driver has quietly stolen the tank-like 1974 Ford Galaxie 500 sedan you see O'Neal in here, and taken it on an exhilarating fling around the night-time city with two petrified casino robbers cowering on the back seat. Another thrilling sequence sees the anti-hero all but destroy a 1970 Mercedes-Benz 280SE in an underground car park. O'Neal plays it cool, although the stunt driver team really deserve more credit than their mentions lost in the textual blur of the end credits allow... (EMI Films/Twentieth Century Fox Film Corporation)

There's so much to enjoy in this image of Samantha Eggar in *The Lady In The Car With Glasses & A Gun*. For one thing, the British actress is actually driving that 1969 Mercury Marquis convertible in character on a busy French *autoroute*, shot directly head-on from the camera car whose open tailgate you can see at the top of the photo. The tense psychological thriller, French made in 1970 (and then re-made in 2015), sees Eggar's character of Dany lose her car to a hitchhiker only to find it again in Marseilles with a gun and a corpse in the boot. Uncredited automotive extras in this still include, to the left, an unusual Citroën articulated car transporter with a cargo of brand-new DS saloons, and to the right a Renault 4 followed by a Renault 10 and then a Citroën 2CV; right up behind the Mercury is an impatient Peugeot 204. (Columbia Pictures Industries Inc)

The American movie staple of cowboys got an urban twist in *The Cowboy Way*, an action comedy where two combative cowboys played by Keifer Sutherland and Woody Harrelson set off for New York. They aim to track down their Latino pal Nacho Salazar, whose daughter has been enslaved in a seedy sweatshop. First they find her, and then they set to around NYC to find the murderer of her father. They have proper Hicksville wheels too, in the form of this well used 1985 Chevrolet C-10 pickup whose dusty red paintwork is flattened by the intense sunlight of its working life back home in New Mexico. (UIP/Universal)

The plot of *The Next Man* is a bit perplexing. It has locations in eight different countries and Sean Connery has a role the like of which he'd never experienced before – as an Arab diplomat called Khalil Abdul-Muhsen from a fictional Middle Eastern state, who is trying to make peace with Israel and admit his country to OPEC. In this 1976 political conspiracy thriller, Abdul-Muhsen travels to New York on his mission, but naturally he becomes the target of a series of assassination attempts. The Arab statesman is chauffeured around the city in a long-wheelbase Mercedes-Benz 600, seen here on the right, which is hardly the least conspicuous car. The motorcade is passing through a protest and that briefcase being reached for by a security man is about to explode with devastating effect, although the marked man actually makes his escape in a different car. (Allied Artists Pictures)

After three successive TV series, Leslie Charteris's justice-seeking adventurer *The Saint* returned to cinema screens for the first time since the 1940s in 1997, with Val Kilmer rebuffing another outing as Bruce Wayne/ Batman to step into the highly polished Chelsea boots made famous by Roger Moore in the 1960s. None of Charteris's numerous old stories were revisited, though, as The Saint aka Simon Templar plunged into a story about Russian mafia attempts to steal nuclear fusion secrets from a beautiful scientist. The action is set in

Moscow with a lot of the intrigue split between Oxford and London, and here is a scene being filmed of The Saint's departure from his ritzy mews house in the British capital. The globally famous TV version of the character from the 1960s was synonymous with the Volvo P1800 used in the show, and Volvo pretty much launched its all-new C70 coupe via an elaborate tie-in with the film. Veteran producer David Brown even turned up at the 1996 Birmingham motor show to help pull the cover off it. (Volvo Car UK Ltd)

Moonrunners was a 1974 B-movie that acted as a dry run for the TV series *The Dukes Of Hazzard*. Both were created by Gy Waldron. And both were set around the running of tax-dodging moonshine liquor and the high-level driving skills, honed in stock car racing, to run it across county lines in the Deep South. Brothers Grady and Bobby Lee Hagg run moonshine for their Uncle Jesse, who prides himself on his old-school methods going right back to the Prohibition era, but the threat builds from New York mobsters who want a piece of the action. Naturally, driving stunt work abounds; here Bobby Lee (Kiel Hagg) has just crashed through the wall of a local bar in a beaten-up but sturdy 1971 Chevrolet Biscayne, one of several used in the film. (United Artists)

On the hunt for an invisible nemesis in *The Amazing Transparent Man*, a 1960 sci-fi B-movie. The gathered law-enforcers are looking to apprehend Joey Faust (Douglas Kennedy), an escaped criminal who's been coerced into stealing money and radioactive material for a mad scientist; the hazardous stuff is being used to feed an invisibility machine that is also giving Joey his cover. Their cars are a fine slice of turn-of-the-decade Detroit metal: on the left is a 1960 Ford Custom 300, in the centre the sharp-edged front end of a 1959 Buick Electra 225, and on the right a 1958 Ford Custom 300. Despite the shoestring budget and far-fetched premise, some of the effects and acting do redeem. (MCP Pictures)

The hunt for a humanoid in a spacesuit intensifies after what appears to have been a flying saucer crash in California's San Fernando Valley. Here the radioactive alien with powers of invisibility is nervous as the Federal Communications Commission search team splits to track him down. *Phantom From Space* was a 1953, independently made B-movie from producer-director F. Lee Wilder at the height of the little-green-men sci-fi craze and the attendant hysteria that cinemagoers loved. There's a great circle of classic Detroit Americana – as well as the alien in his spacesuit – in this still. Leading the search for the radio-wave-scrambling invader is the 1947 Ford Super Deluxe station wagon complete with its roof-mounted detector antenna, middle right; below that is a handsome 1952 Dodge Coronet; and to its left, hidden by the building and the spaceman, the nose of a 1949 Plymouth Special Deluxe Station Wagon. The real rarity is the 1953 Kaiser Manhattan sedan far left, and then to its right there's a 1952 Ford Ranch Wagon. (Budd Rodgers)

Alex Rogan (Lance Guest) is a video-gaming whizz-kid whose life and bleak prospects on a trailer park whirl away from him after he meets Centauri, apparently a computer games executive who created the *Starfighter* game that Alex has totally mastered. But before he knows it, Alex is spun off into a virtual world where he is battling to save the galaxy from evil forces 'for real'. This entailed journeying through space in a flying car. Teen sci-fi fans might have felt there was something eerily familiar about this gullwing-door, wedge-shaped contraption, and not

merely its vague similarity to the DeLorean DMC-12. An earlier iteration of the 'Starcar' had appeared in *Blade Runner* two years before *The Last Starfighter* was released, and both were the work of fabled Hollywood car builder Gene Winfield. It existed both in Volkswagen-powered full size for filming, as here, and in digital computer-generated form. The three-dimensional one was not broken up, like so many automotive movie props, but is thought to be in a private collection in France, and now painted red. (Lorimar/Universal Pictures)